YEAR C
AFTER PENTECOST 1

YEAR C
AFTER PENTECOST 1

PREACHING
THE REVISED
COMMON
LECTIONARY

Marion Soards
Thomas Dozeman
Kendall McCabe

ABINGDON PRESS
Nashville

PREACHING THE REVISED COMMON LECTIONARY
YEAR C: AFTER PENTECOST 1

Copyright © 1994 by Abingdon Press

This book is printed on recycled, acid-free paper.

Library of Congress Cataloging-in-Publication Data
(Revised for vol. 3)

Soards, Marion L., 1952–
    Preaching the Revised common lectionary : year C.

    Includes indexes.
    Contents: [1] Advent/Christmas/Epiphany —
[2] Lent/Easter — [3] After Pentecost 1.
    1. Lectionary preaching. 2. Bible—Homiletical use. I. Dozeman, Thomas B.
II. McCabe, Kendall, 1939–   . III. Title. IV. Title: Common lectionary (1992)
BV4235.L43S63   1994   251   93-30550
ISBN 0-687-33804-2 (v. 1 : alk. paper)
ISBN 0-687-33805-0 (v. 2 : alk. paper)
ISBN 0-687-33806-9 (v. 3 : alk. paper)

Scripture quotations, unless otherwise noted, are from the New Revised Standard Version of the Bible, copyright © 1989 by the Division of Christian Education of the National Council of the Churches of Christ in the USA. Used by permission.

Scripture quotations marked AP are the author's paraphrase of the Bible.

94 95 96 97 98 99 00 01 02 03 — 10 9 8 7 6 5 4 3 2 1

MANUFACTURED IN THE UNITED STATES OF AMERICA

Contents

CONTENTS

This is one volume in a twelve-volume series. Each volume contains commentary and worship suggestions for a portion of the lectionary cycle A, B, or C. Since the lections for a few special days do not change from one lectionary cycle to another, material for each of these days appears in only one of the volumes. Appropriate cross references in the table of contents lead the reader to material in other volumes of the series.

Introduction

Now pastors and students have a systematic treatment of essential issues of the Christian year and Bible study for worship and proclamation based on the Revised Common Lectionary. Interpretation of the lectionary will separate into three parts: Calendar, Canon, and Celebration. A brief word of introduction will provide helpful guidelines for utilizing this resource in worship through the Christian year.

Calendar. Every season of the Christian year will be introduced with a theological interpretation of its meaning, and how it relates to the overall Christian year. This section will also include specific liturgical suggestions for the season.

Canon. The lectionary passages will be interpreted in terms of their setting, structure, and significance. First, the word *setting* is being used loosely in this commentary to include a range of different contexts in which biblical texts can be interpreted from literary setting to historical or cultic settings. Second, regardless of how the text is approached under the heading of setting, interpretation will always proceed to an analysis of the structure of the text under study. Third, under the heading of significance, central themes and motifs of the passage will be underscored to provide a theological interpretation of the text as a springboard for preaching. Thus interpretation of the lectionary passages will result in the outline on the next page.

Celebration. This section will focus on specific ways of relating the lessons to liturgical acts and/or homiletical options for the day on which they occur. How the texts have been used in the Christian tradition will sometimes be illustrated to stimulate the thinking of preachers and planners of worship services.

I. OLD TESTAMENT TEXTS

A. The Old Testament Lesson

1. Setting

2. Structure

3. Significance

B. Psalm

1. Setting

2. Structure

3. Significance

II. NEW TESTAMENT TEXTS

A. The Epistle

1. Setting

2. Structure

3. Significance

B. The Gospel

1. Setting

2. Structure

3. Significance

Why We Use the Lectionary

Although many denominations have been officially or unofficially using some form of the lectionary for many years, some pastors are still unclear about where it comes from, why some lectionaries differ from denomination to denomination, and why the use of a lectionary is to be preferred to a more random sampling of scripture.

Simply put, the use of a lectionary provides a more diverse scriptural diet for God's people, and it can help protect the congregation from the whims and prejudices of the pastor and other worship planners. Faithful use of the lectionary means that preachers must deal with texts they had rather ignore, but about which the congregation may have great concern and interest. The healing of Naaman in the Jordan, which we encounter in this volume at Proper 9, might be a case in point. Adherence to the lectionary can be an antidote to that homiletical arrogance that says, "I know what my people need," and in humility acknowledges that the Word of God found in scripture may speak to more needs on Sunday morning than we even know exist, when we seek to proclaim faithfully the message we have wrestled from the text.

The lectionary may also serve as a resource for liturgical content. The psalm is intended to be a response to the Old Testament lesson, and not read as a lesson itself, but beyond that the lessons may inform the content of prayers of confession, intercession, and petition. Some lessons may be adapted as affirmations of faith, as in *The United Methodist Hymnal,* nos. 887-89; the United Church of Christ's *Hymnal,* nos. 429-30; and the Presbyterian *Worshipbook,* no. 30. The "Celebration" entries for each day will call attention to these opportunities from time to time.

Pastors and preachers in the free-church tradition should think of the lectionary as a primary resource for preaching and worship, but need to remember that the lectionary was made for them and not they for the lectionary. The lectionary may serve as the inspiration for a separate series of lessons and sermons that will include texts not in the present edition, or having chosen one of the lectionary passages as the basis for the day's sermon, the preacher may wish to make an independent choice of the other lessons to supplement and illustrate the primary text. The lectionary will be of most value when its use is not a cause for legalism but for inspiration. Pastors who experience a love/hate relationship with the lectionary will gain much sympathy and guidance from Eugene Lowry's penetrating analysis in *Living with the Lectionary: Preaching Through the Revised Common Lectionary* (Nashville: Abingdon Press, 1992).

Just as there are no perfect preachers, there are no perfect lectionaries. The Revised Common Lectionary, upon which this series is based, is the result of the work of many years by the Consultation on Common Texts and is a response to ongoing evaluation of the Common Lectionary (1983) by pastors and scholars from the several participating denominations. The current interest in the lectionary can be traced back to the Second Vatican Council, which ordered lectionary revision for the Roman Catholic Church:

> The treasures of the Bible are to be opened up more lavishly, so that richer fare may be provided for the faithful at the table of God's Word. In this way a more representative portion of the holy Scriptures will be read to the people over a set cycle of years. (*The Documents of Vatican II*, Walter Abbott, ed. [Piscataway, N.J.: New Century, 1974], p. 155)

The example thus set by Roman Catholics inspired Protestants to take more seriously the place of the Bible in their services and sermons, and soon many denominations had issued their own three-year cycles, based generally on the Roman Catholic model, but with their own modifications. This explains why some discrepancies and variations appear in different forms of the lectionary. The Revised Common Lectionary (RCL) is an effort to increase agreement among the churches. A table at the end of the volume will list the differences among the RCL and the Roman Catholic, Episcopal, and Lutheran lectionaries. Where no entry is made, all are in agreement with the RCL.

For those unacquainted with the general pattern of the lectionary, a brief word of explanation may be helpful for sermon preparation.

(1) The three years are each distinguished by one of the Synoptic Gospels: Matthew in A, Mark in B, Luke in C. John is distributed over the three years with a heavy emphasis during Lent and Easter. (2) Two types of readings are used. During the periods of Advent to Epiphany and Lent to Pentecost, the readings are usually topical—that is, there is some common theme among them. During the Sundays after Epiphany and Pentecost the readings are continuous, with no necessary connection between the lessons. In the period covered by this volume, there is a thematic connection between the Old Testament lesson and the Gospel during the Sundays after Epiphany, but the epistle lesson begins a continuous reading from Galatians. The preacher begins, then, with at least four preaching options: to deal with either one of the lessons on their own or to work with the dialogue between the Old Testament lesson and the Gospel. Perhaps it should also be added that though the psalm is intended to be a response by the people to the Old Testament lesson—rather than as a lesson on its own—this in no way suggests that it cannot be used as the text for the sermon.

This is the third of four volumes that will deal with the lessons for the entire C Cycle of the Christian year. The first volume covered Advent through the Sundays after Epiphany. The second volume included Ash Wednesday through the Day of Pentecost. This volume begins with Trinity Sunday (the First Sunday After Pentecost) and includes all the lessons for June, July, and August. The fourth volume finishes the remainder of the year, including the lessons for All Saints' Day (November 1). Years A and B have been published previously, also in two series of four volumes each.

A note on language: We have used the term *Old Testament* in this series because that is the language employed by the Consultation on Common Texts, at least up to this point. Pastors and worship committees may wish to consider alternative terms, such as *First Testament* or *Hebrew Scriptures,* that do not imply that those writings somehow have less value than the rest of the Christian Bible. Another option is to refer to *First Lesson* (always from the Hebrew Scriptures), *Second Lesson* (from Acts, Revelation, or the epistles), and *Gospel.*

SUMMER SUNDAY PREACHING IN PENTECOST

Few preachers apparently look forward to that long expanse of Sundays reaching from Trinity Sunday to Labor Day. Summer is a time for planning what will happen after Labor Day, and for vacations. Father's Day, the Fourth, and Labor Day Sunday are not high holy days on the calendars of most local churches. At most, these events are blips on the liturgical screen. Indeed, two months intervene between Independence Day and Labor Day, and the preacher's imagination is taxed to find ways in which to make service and sermon "meaningful." This creative breakdown has been known to result in various kinds of experimental and innovative liturgies and sermons—which, if they fail, make no listener feel too badly, since they were in the nature of a trial balloon or an attention getter. They perhaps provide sufficient justification for defining liturgical reform as that which is intended to save the people of God from the clever ideas of the leadership!

Into this dilemma comes the lectionary as a means of introducing what might seem to be a revolutionary concept in many places—reading, studying, and celebrating the scriptural witness in a consecutive way over a sustained period of time. To appreciate why the key word here is *consecutive,* it is necessary to understand the overall structure of the lectionary.

During the "proper" times of the year, Advent to Epiphany and Ash Wednesday to Pentecost, the lessons are generally chosen so as to have some kind of thematic connection, drawing together varied scriptural witnesses to help us gain insight into the meaning of the sacred mystery being anticipated or celebrated. Volumes 1 and 2 in this series illustrate that pattern. Even the "ordinary" Sundays between Epiphany and Ash Wednesday have the Old Testament lessons chosen in relation to the day's Gospel which, with the epistle, is being read sequentially. But when we come to the ordinary time after Pentecost, the lessons operate on three independent tracks with no intentional thematic relationship between them.

13

(Note that the term *ordinary time*, does not mean "not special." It derives from the Latin word for "order," and refers to the fact that these Sundays are simply numbered in sequence in the Roman Catholic lectionary without reference to being "after Epiphany" or "after Pentecost.")

In Year C, the ruling Gospel is Luke, the evangelist who displays a great concern for the poor and underprivileged and demonstrates Christ's compassion for them from his birth in a borrowed crib to his death in company with criminals. On the Sundays covered by this volume, we begin with Jesus at dinner rebuking Simon the Pharisee for his prejudice against the woman who anointed Jesus' feet, and we conclude at another meal with Jesus teaching us to entertain those who cannot repay us. Thus the Old Testament lessons after Pentecost are intended to recall for us the ethical content of the prophetic witness in ancient Israel. They begin with Elijah's judgment upon Ahab for the misuse of his authority in taking Naboth's vineyard and they continue with other readings from Amos and Hosea, prophets particularly known for their outcry against social injustice. The intent is not that there be a one-on-one thematic connection between the two readings, but rather that the Old Testament lessons keep us aware of the prophetic context and tradition within which Jesus lived and out of which he preached. The epistle texts, by reminding us of the priority of faith in Christian experience, guard us against the self-righteousness that an emphasis on social justice alone might engender.

The lectionary creators intend that the order of reading be Old Testament, psalm response, epistle, Gospel. The psalm is a response to the Old Testament reading, not a lesson in itself (though that does not mean it cannot be used as the text for the sermon, since it is a part of the canon). This use of the psalter as a resource for prayer and praise reminds us of our roots in synagogue and the Temple. In the epistle, we hear the apostolic witness, which understands itself to be in continuity with the work of God in the experience of Israel in the Old Testament and sees itself as a fulfillment of God's promise to Israel. The Gospel is read last, because that is the vehicle through which the community interprets both the experience of Israel and the primitive Church. There is a kind of historical development here, since usually each reading is older in time than the one following it, but this is no justification for the pattern. The rationale is unabashedly christological. It is through Christ that we view and interpret both the witness of the Old Testament and the apostles. It is for this reason that in many traditions the congregation stands to hear the Gospel read—not because the Gospels are somehow "better" scripture, but because they are an icon of Christ in our midst, and it is Christ whom we stand to greet.

This means that the order of the lessons is not changed so that the one with the primary text is closest to the sermon, because we still need the word of Christ through which to focus our attention. Even if, in ordinary time, the Gospel does not relate thematically to either of the previous lessons, it is still the last lesson because of the symbolic lesson to be learned. It may be that there is a particular Gospel lesson that the preacher has used as a vehicle for interpreting one of the earlier lessons. That may provide a justification for changing the Gospel of the day in order to establish the thematic connection. For example, Proper 9 has as the Old Testament lesson the story of the healing of Namaan the leper. The Gospel is the account of the commissioning of the seventy in chapter 10, a rich mine for preaching, but difficult to relate to Namaan. The preacher should feel free to change the Gospel for the day to Luke 5:12-16, the story of Jesus healing a leper. Parallels should be immediately apparent to the homilitician. This decision maintains the priority of Luke, and it provides a reading not otherwise included in the lectionary. Paul's reference in the epistle reading to the new creation may provide an interpretive perspective from which to view the other two lessons.

This kind of creative and critical thinking allows for an expansion of the lectionary by the insightful preacher if each set is taken in turn each three years as the governing lesson. The preacher then makes other thematic choices (assuming the integrity of the texts is maintained). Already one's preaching ministry has developed possibilities for the next nine years and mitigates the accusation that the lectionary limits the preacher's choice of texts.

In recent years, the dictum that the text and the sermon should not be separated has become a kind of mantra that has given rise to a new liturgical legalism that does not understand the liturgical setting out of which the dictum originated. The reason for the rule is not to disallow a hymn between lesson and sermon (or even two lessons with responses). It grows out of the practice, still current in some places, of having the (one and only) Scripture lesson very early on in the service, followed by a pastoral prayer, an anthem, the offering, the announcements, a hymn, and whatever else, and then finally the sermon. The dictum is intended to prevent this kind of separation that so isolates the reading of the Scripture from the preaching of the Word that the two are rarely related in the minds of the hearers.

Though it may be called "ordinary" time, it is still *kairos* with which we are dealing, and for the Christian time is always a vehicle for grace. Ideally, the lectionary creators intend that there be a convergence of the Word of the Lord with the Supper of the Lord on the Day of the Lord. The dismemberment of these elements in practice has led to a diminished identity on the part of the Christian community. The Word without the Supper becomes as breath without body, because it denies the incarnational principle enunciated in John 1, which is at the heart of the Christian revelation. No less tragic is the celebration of the Supper without the proclamation of the Word, which gives us a body without breath. And equally tragic is the confusion of the Sabbath with the Lord's Day. It is often easier to observe the Sabbath with its negations than to live with the scandalous joy and grace that characterize life in the kingdom.

During ordinary time we are challenged by what to do with Easter, since it is responsible for the whole enterprise that is the Christian Church. Easter is the formative event for Christians, the eighth day of the new creation, the day that reminds us that we die, are buried, and then raised with Christ. As a result, our view of the world will henceforth be slightly skewed, since we are learning to look at life from the other side of the Resurrection. Proper time is rather straightforward as we hear again the ancient narratives, remember "the old, old story," and rejoice at our incorporation into the mighty acts of God. But ordinary time is no time to act as though all of that never happened! On the contrary, ordinary time is the setting for applying Easter to make life extraordinary. Galatians can give us a model this summer (as can others of Paul's letters at other times). Paul's great theological treatise on Christian faith and freedom concludes with a series of admonitions about Christian living in consequence of our freedom obtained through the cross (Proper 9). The question always before us during ordinary time is, What do we do about Easter? The lessons suggest resources in our search for answers as they portray a Christ who practiced open communion (Proper 6), rebuked retributive attitudes and actions (Proper 8), condemned the inhospitable (Proper 9), and radically redefined the meaning of neighbor two thousand years before we spoke of being a global village (Proper 10).

The former pattern for counting the days in the Christian year always spoke of days "After Pentecost" or "After Trinity," and the tendency then was to think of that time as "the season of Pentecost." Both lectionary and calendar reform have recovered the primitive understanding that the Day of Pentecost is part of Easter, the Great Fifty Days, and that resurrection and empowerment by the Spirit are inseparable (see commentary in Year C, Lent and Easter of this series). We live empowered by the Spirit of the risen Christ, and so as Colossians says (Proper 13), we are now about the business of seeking the things that are above, and that has implications for how we go about the business of living here below. The preacher's exciting challenge this and every summer is to engage the congregation in dialogue about what it means to love God and do as you please!

The standard color for ordinary time is green. In order to avoid tedium and monotony during these six months, a variety of greens and summer colors might be used along with fresh flowers from local gardens. The readings for the day may also present ideas for different kinds of visuals from Sunday to Sunday.

Trinity Sunday (First Sunday After Pentecost)

Old Testament Texts

Proverbs 8:1-4, 22-31 is a speech about creation by Wisdom personified. Psalm 8 is apparently a hymn of praise that celebrates the creative power of God.

The Lesson: Proverbs 8:1-4, 22-31

The Authority of Wisdom

Setting. Wisdom is personified in the Old Testament lesson as a woman. This is the second time in the book of Proverbs that such a personification takes place. In Proverbs 1:20-33 the woman Wisdom was pictured as calling out to persons in the marketplace to pay attention to her. See the commentary for Year B, Proper 19 for interpretation of this text. The personification of Wisdom in Proverbs 8 repeats this picture of a woman calling out to encourage those who may hear her to embrace the power of her teaching in vv. 5-21. The Old Testament lesson, however, has excluded these verses, and thus focuses less on the calling out of Wisdom to humans, and more on the identity (and hence authority) of Wisdom herself. The authority of Wisdom is explored in Proverbs 8:1-4, 22-31 by describing the relationship between Wisdom and God.

Structure. Proverbs 8 separates into the following sections. Verses 1-3 provide the setting for the discourse of Wisdom. It is in the midst of everyday life: the text underscores how she is positioned at the crossroads, by the gates, in front of the town. Verse 4 firmly establishes humans as the object of her discourse: "To you O people, I call, and my cry is to all that live." Verse 4 most likely introduces a section that continues through v. 11, where humans in the marketplace are admonished to listen to Wisdom's call. Verses 12-21 shift from direct admonishing of humans to a series of "I" statements by Wisdom, which focus on the power of her advice to influence human action. These statements provide insight into the identity of Wisdom from a human point of view. This section is not included in the lectionary reading, but the preacher may want to take note of the content in this section, for it leads into the next section, vv. 22-31, which is the central portion of the lectionary reading. Verses 22-31 also explore the identity of Wisdom, but from a divine point of view by describing the creation of Wisdom prior to creation. Here the focus is not the relationship of Wisdom to humans as in vv. 12-21, but the relationship of Wisdom to God. Finally, vv. 32-36 conclude the chapter by returning to a speech of encouragement or admonition by Wisdom that is once again directed to humans in much the same manner as vv. 4-11.

The structure of Proverbs 8 can be summarized in five parts. After the introduction establishes the setting (vv. 1-3), two direct addresses by Wisdom to humans (vv. 4-11 and 32-36) frame two sections in which Wisdom identifies herself. Verses 12-21 explore the identity of Wisdom from a human point of view ("I, wisdom, live with prudence, and I attain knowledge and discretion"). Verses 22-31 explore the identity of Wisdom from a divine point of view by exploring her birth and her relationship to God prior to creation ("The LORD created me at the beginning of his work"). This summary illustrates how the chapter is constructed as a pyramid, with God at the top and humans at the bottom, while Wisdom provides a link between them. The admonishing of Wisdom in the marketplace in vv. 4-11 and 32-36 is at the very bottom of the pyramid. These speeches take place in the everyday nitty-gritty of life. When Wisdom shifts the focus from a direct admonition of humans in order to make identity statements about herself in vv. 12-21, the text moves one step away from the immediate give-and-take of the marketplace. Verses 22-31 take yet another step away from the marketplace, when Wisdom describes her birth prior to creation and her relationship to God. Even though the speeches move away from the immediacy of the marketplace, they are certainly not detached from the early admonitions. In fact, one could argue that vv. 22-31 carry the weight of the entire chapter, for they are meant to provide the authority for Wisdom's voice in the marketplace. Our interpretation must explore what is the authority of Wisdom.

Significance. A pivotal distinction is made in vv. 22-31 between Wisdom and creation. Creation in these verses is a process by which God limits other things or objects much like a craftsman. Creation, in this case, includes the shaping of mountains (v. 25), circling the deep (v. 27), firming up the skies (v. 28), limiting the sea (v. 29), and marking out the foundations of the earth (v. 29). Many of these images call to mind mythological traditions in which God's creative power is seen in the context of conflict with different forces of chaos. One is reminded of the Babylonian creation mythology, *Enuma Elish,* where the God Marduk fashions creation out of the body of the watery chaos goddess, Tiamat; or perhaps the Canaanite god Baal, who struggles with Yamm, the sea God. Creation in such contexts must be understood as the ability of God to restore order from these fundamentally chaotic forces, and in imposing order, God fashions a world. In such mythology there are secrets in the substructure of creation, where hidden boundaries have been established, of which humans know nothing. Creation in Proverbs 8 is being conceived to some degree in this same way.

Wisdom, however, is not part of this process of creation. First, note all the time words that are used in vv. 22-25 to locate Wisdom prior to this creative activity of God (for example, "long ago," "ages ago," "at the first," "before the beginning"). Second, the origin of Wisdom is conceived of as a birth, rather than as the product of divine craftsmanship. In v. 22 Wisdom states that God created her either "as the beginning of his way" or "at the beginning of his way." (The NRSV translates this verse, "The LORD created me at the beginning of his work.") The Hebrew word that is translated as create *(qanah)* carries the imagery of procreation or birth. The verse suggests that God gave birth to Wisdom as compared to the rest of creation, which came into existence by God's activity as a craftsman. Wisdom's relationship to God, therefore, is very different from all other powers in creation. Verse 30 makes reference to this relationship. The NRSV translates the verse as follows: "then I was beside him, like a master worker; and

I was daily his delight." This translation attributes some activity of creation to Wisdom herself through the image of "master worker" (Hebrew, 'amon). The meaning of this word is debated, and it might also be translated "darling," in which case Wisdom is describing herself as God's child (hence the early imagery to procreation in v. 22), and stating how she provided God with daily delight.

Two important points emerge for preaching this text. The first point concerns the authority of Wisdom. Her authority does not rest in her ability to create. Rather her authority arises from the fact that as God's begotten child, she witnessed all the intricacies of creation as they were taking place, with the result that she now knows all the hidden secrets that are buried into the fabric of creation. Furthermore, there is no one else besides God who knows these secrets. Obviously her teaching is worth heeding.

The second point that is worthy of preaching concerns the relationship between Wisdom and God. The obscurity of the text (note the problems of translation in vv. 22 and 30) underscores how the authors are probing the very limits of their ability to talk about God. The text, however, suggests that Wisdom is personified and indeed divinized to some degree. She was begotten and not created, hence her relationship to God is qualitatively different from all other powers in creation. The force of this claim is not in the metaphysical speculation that such claims may prompt in how we think about God. Rather the power of this claim is most strongly felt when we remind ourselves of the setting of Proverbs 8. This divinized personality, who played with God before creation, is standing in the marketplace during rush hour nearly begging passersby to let her tell them the secrets of creation. This is the astonishing message of the text. Wisdom is not only able to bridge the large gap between humans and God, but she is out in the marketplace trying to give away God's secrets. The problem is in getting anyone to listen to her.

The Response: *Psalm 8*

What Are Humans?

Setting. Psalm 8 is a hymn of praise that modulates between an individual voice (vv. 1b-8) and a community refrain (vv. 1b, 9). The central motif of the community refrain is the celebration of the name of God.

Structure. Psalm 8 separates into two sections: vv. 1-4 and 5-9. The community refrain begins the first section (v. 1*b*) and concludes the last section (v. 9), with the result that the praise of God's name throughout the earth frames the entire psalm. The voice of the individual singer takes up the middle portion of the psalm. Within this section, the central theme of the psalm appears to be the question of v. 4: "What are human beings that you are mindful of them?" Most commentators agree that this question and the description of the role of humans in creation that follows in vv. 6-8 is based on the account of creation of humans in Genesis 1:26. Thus Psalm 8 should be read as inner-biblical reflection on Genesis 1.

Significance. Psalm 8 is somewhat unusual in that it is a hymn of praise that addresses God in the second person ("you"). The use of the second person establishes a certain intimacy in the relationship between singer and God, which is striking because it contrasts with the vast (and impersonal) creation imagery that is the subject matter of much of the hymn (God is sovereign, majestic, creator of heavens, moon and stars, etc.). This contrast between the intimate relationship of singer and God, on the one hand, and the vastness of the creation order, on the other, is an important point of entry into interpreting Psalm 8, for it provides the background for the central question in v. 4. What are humans to God in the larger context of the universe? On such a larger stage our first response would be that humans are insignificant to the larger drama of creation. Psalm 8 is a hymn of praise because just the opposite is true. God is not only mindful of earthbound mortals (v. 4), but he has even given them a formative role as actors on the large stage of creation. One suspects that this paradox (between the insignificance of humans in the larger order of creation and the degree of attention that God bestows on them) may provide insight for interpreting v. 2, which has no parallel any place in Scripture. Perhaps it is the frail human mortals who are the babes of v. 2 that God has chosen as a defense against evil, even though God had so many more resources at his disposal: "You have set your glory above the heavens." The imagery of Wisdom begging for a hearing in the market underscores the extreme limits that God is willing to go to include humans in the management of creation. This fact is what prompts the wonder and awe of the psalmist concerning the position of humans in the larger drama of God's creation.

New Testament Texts

The texts were chosen for their use of Trinitarian-like language. But preachers should remind themselves that the verses of both readings are a starting point for Trinitarian thinking. The biblical authors wrote prior to later doctrinal discussions, although their texts were crucial points of reference for the later more developed ideas that subsequently guided the thought and life of the Church.

The Epistle: *Romans 5:1-5*

On Relating to the Fullness of God

Setting. The dominant concern of chapters 5–8 is the life of the Christian community, especially in its experience of grace. The first four chapters of Romans were concerned with the righteousness of God and the sin of humankind, Jews and Gentiles, law and faith; and these themes were developed through a series of exegetical arguments. A turn from theological juxtapositions and exegetical explanations began in 4:23-25; and now in chapter 5 we find Paul meditating overtly on the nature and significance of Christian existence in this world. The previous polemic and dialectic yields to an essentially straightforward (for Paul!) celebration of grace.

Structure. In vv. 1-5 Paul declares our (assuming that in worship we take our stand with the Romans and not at a distance as mere observers) justification and expands upon that important idea. There is a clear theological cast to Paul's thought. First, faith in relation to Christ yields peace with God as Jesus Christ is Lord—that is, recognition and obedience to the authority of Christ overcomes the distance between God and ourselves. Through Christ we have access to divine grace and, thus, we hope for the experience of God's glory. Moreover, faith and grace transform our lives so that despite real difficulties we live in hope because of God's love that is present and powerful in the person of the Holy Spirit.

Significance. One is tempted to do a series of word studies in relation to this passage, since it is loaded with significant theological terminology. Such a tactic may unpack much of the meaning of this text, but it will also render Paul's thinking fairly static, whereas in fact he is expressing the dynamic quality of Christian life in these verses. Thus, we need to create a sense of motion in reflecting on this passage that will impart some of Paul's own energy to our congregations.

Paul starts with the present, saying that we are justified by faith (literally, Paul speaks spatially, not instrumentally, saying "we are justified out of faith"). Being justified in theological terms is like being justified in typing or printing; it means that everything has been set into a proper line. Christians are neither ragged right nor ragged left, we are justified. Actually, we have been justified—that is, God has set us into the right relationship with God's self through Jesus Christ. Thus, our justification is grace! This good news puts us at peace, because, Paul says, we have (through being justified) access to grace. But this experience of the goodness of God is neither static nor complete, for the apostle immediately talks of our hope. Hope is related to our future, which has been created by the gracious work of God in Jesus Christ. For Paul, this scheme is far from "possibility thinking"; rather, it is "reality living." And so Paul continues his meditation by bringing us all down into the swamps of life—suffering. Yet, look how Paul can speak of suffering. He does not deny its reality. He does not glorify it. Instead he puts a good face on it by relating it to endurance and character-building. Oddly, the outcome of our suffering, which produces endurance and builds character, is that we hope. Paul has taken us for a ride in a logical loop: We rejoice in our hope that allows us to rejoice in our suffering, which yields endurance and increases character and produces hope. Christian existence, created by grace, is set in motion after hope, which is not yet fully realized, but which is already present in a preliminary way. Paul says we live as we do because God's own love is poured into our hearts by the Holy Spirit.

Of course, these verses were chosen for reading and preaching on Trinity Sunday because of the mention of God, Christ, and the Holy Spirit. Yet, notice that the text is not primarily a lesson about the

Holy Trinity, especially in ontological terms. Throughout these lines we see Paul's concern for the actual transformation of our lives. Essentially Paul declares that we have been brought into a new, graciously-given, and faithfully-formed relationship to God through the lordship of Christ and the presence of the Holy Spirit. This relationship, however, is crucial for the living of our everyday lives. Paul does not think here of a spirituality that is removed from or merely transcendent of our existence. Rather, Christians live altered lives because of a new relationship to God. Because of this new relationship, we are able to endure suffering, even viewing it positively (although Paul is not saying that suffering is good) because of our hope in God.

The Gospel: *John 16:12-15*

The Mediation of God's Truth

Setting. Recognizing the general context in which this lesson occurs is crucial for grasping the importance of the lines. Earlier in the Gospel (13:1), John signaled a move out of the so-called Book of Signs (John 1–12) and into the so-called Book of Glory (13–20 [21?]) with the overt statement that Jesus recognized that his "hour" had come; in turn, the supernatural significance of the time was signaled by the report concerning the activity of "the devil" in John 13:2. In this setting, on the day before Passover, Jesus and his disciples took a meal together. During or after the meal Jesus washed the disciples' feet. Conversation on washing, humility, and love followed, along with Jesus' troubled prediction that Judas would betray him. Jesus dismissed Judas from the gathering, and when he had gone Jesus began to speak to the disciples. After a brief exchange with Simon Peter, Jesus eventually spoke at great length to his followers.

Our lesson comes from a portion of the section of the Book of Signs known as "the Last Discourse" (14:1–17:26). Some scholars refer to this speech as Jesus' "last will and testament." His words are not those of a dead man, however; rather they inform the disciples (and the readers of John!) in detail of the identity and intentions of the crucified, risen, and exalted Lord. In the verses of our lesson

Jesus speaks of the Spirit and the Father, so that the verses seem appropriate for Trinity Sunday.

Structure. Although the lesson is only four verses, it is filled with crucial concepts, which, in their expression, lend complexity to the structure of the reading. First, in v. 12 Jesus makes an opening statement that contrasts the limits of the present time in which he and the disciples stand with the promised future, and in which there will be further divine revelation. Second, vv. 13-14 raise the important topic of the coming of the Spirit of Truth. The role of the Spirit is defined in a series of statements about authority for teaching, the source of truth, and the purpose of the Spirit's work. Third, in near-poetry v. 15 declares the essential unity of God the Father, Jesus the Son, and the Spirit. The three are mutually involved with the Father's will and word. Moreover, that which the Father gave to Jesus, the Spirit will give to Jesus' followers. Careful study of the particular contents of these verses and the logical arrangement of their presentation may prove helpful in designing a sermon related to these challenging lines.

Significance. Perhaps the final verse of this lesson provides a helpful starting point for preaching on Trinity Sunday. Here we learn that while all that God has belongs to Jesus, the Son, the role of the Spirit at work in the life of the community of faith is to deliver faithfully that which belongs to the Son (and to the Father) to the Son's followers. The focus here is on the Spirit as teacher of the disciples of Christ. Remarkably, there will be nothing new in this teaching, for it is a faithful communication in keeping with the basic teaching that Jesus himself did—although he taught in a limited fashion in accordance with the capacity of the disciples to hear and learn. Yet, there is genuine continuity from the beginning in the teaching of Jesus through the course of the work of the Spirit and to the completion of that work.

What the community will learn from the Spirit is consistent with what the community began to learn from Christ. Thus, the community can judge the validity and appropriateness of "new" teaching by asking whether it is in keeping with the foundation laid by Christ himself. Moreover, the Spirit of Truth brings glory to Christ and, by implication, to the Father (since all comes ultimately from the

Father), not to the Spirit himself. Teaching that claims inspiration is necessarily focused away from the one doing the teaching and specifically on Christ. This standard is the Church's hermeneutical device for discerning truth.

This seemingly abstract discourse has important, concrete implications for Christians in all ages. First, Christ himself laid a foundation upon which the continuing work of the Spirit in the life of the Church builds. No new foundations will be laid; thus, efforts to redefine Christianity in terms of new contemporary sensibilities are to be tested in terms of continuity with the teaching of Christ. Second, Christ himself is our window to God. Because Christ is the Son and God is the Father, to see the Son is to catch a revealing glimpse of the Father; their relationship is the basis of Christ's capacity to reveal God. Third, the work of the Spirit draws believers into the mix. God in Christ reaches out to humanity, and now the Spirit continues that work of revelation and saving love.

Finally, in the cultural currents of today, the Father-Son paradigm may cause problems for communication. The challenge is to be faithful to the sense of this text without offending or without abandoning the important teaching it offers. Modalist models (such as Creator, Redeemer, and Sanctifier) should be avoided; and preachers should recognize that in actuality pluralistic congregations as many believers will be put off by attempts to revamp Father-Son language as will be helped by the effort to eliminate illegitimate male-dominant biases. The text is about relationships, living relationships, and about God's reaching out to humanity in Christ and the Spirit to give us life.

Trinity Sunday: The Celebration

Dorothy Sayers concludes her play, *The Zeal of Thy House*, with the following speech by St. Michael the Archangel:

> Children of men, lift up your hearts. Laud and magnify God, the everlasting Wisdom, the holy, undivided and adorable Trinity. Praise Him that He hath made man in His own image, a maker and craftsman like Himself, a little mirror of His triune majesty.
>
> For every work of creation is threefold, an earthly trinity to match the heavenly.

First: there is the Creative Idea; passionless, timeless, beholding the whole work complete at once, the end in the beginning; and this is the image of the Father.

Second: there is the Creative Energy, begotten of that Idea, working in time from the beginning to the end, with sweat and passion, being incarnate in the bonds of matter; and this is the image of the Word.

Third: there is the Creative Power, the meaning of the work and its response in the lively soul; and this is the image of the indwelling Spirit.

And these three are one, each equally in itself the whole work, whereof none can exist without other; and this is the image of the Trinity. (*The Zeal of Thy House,* Dorothy L. Sayers [New York: Harcourt, Brace, 1937], pp. 114-15)

This passage may be used in conjunction with the lessons from Proverbs and Romans to talk about what it means to engage in Trinitarian living ("reality living" in the Romans commentary above) when we take seriously the trinitarian character that is ours by virtue of having been created in the image of God who is Trinity. The goal of the sermon is not to convince people of the doctrine of the Trinity as a fact about God; rather, it is to help them see how the Trinity is reflected in their own natures because God made them.

In her theological essay, *The Mind of the Maker* (San Francisco: Harper & Row, 1979), Sayers stresses the importance of an equal balance between "Idea," "Energy," and "Power" and discusses what happens when one is stronger than the others. It is helpful to apply what she says to the creation of sermons. Those who are "father-ridden" are impressed with an Idea and they seek to impose it on others with no consideration of how the particular idea may be most effectively communicated to a particular congregation. There is no "sweat and passion" that will make the idea become "incarnate in the bonds of matter." Those who are "son-ridden" are those who believe that the style of the sermon is paramount, "the prestidigitators of verbal arabesque" who "enjoy a kind of false Pentecost, thrilling and moving the senses but producing no genuine rebirth of the spirit." And those who are "ghost-ridden" so believe in the sufficiency of their own emotions to awaken a response that they neglect the "discipline of a thorough incarnation" and lack "the coherence

29

that derives from reference to a controlling idea." During the coming three months when preachers are beginning to outline their sermon plans for the next year, they might wish to keep Sayers' criteria as a guide for their own creative work:

1. Does the sermon have a controlling idea?
2. Is it expressed in a way (words and style) which will communicate clearly?
3. Does it reflect their own passionate involvement in the idea?

The above speech from *The Zeal of Thy House* could be adapted for use as a call to worship or an affirmation of faith. If it is printed, acknowledgment to Sayers should be noted in the bulletin.

Proper Six
Sunday Between
June 12 and 18 Inclusive
(If After Trinity Sunday)

Old Testament Texts

I Kings 21:1-21a is the story of how queen Jezebel persuaded king Ahab to seize Naboth's vineyard. Psalm 5:1-8 is an individual lament or prayer song.

The Lesson: *I Kings 21:1-21a*

Power

Setting. I Kings 21 is loosely woven into the series of stories that trace the confrontation between the prophet Elijah and king Ahab. This sequence of stories is introduced in I Kings 17 when Elijah bursts on the scene from nowhere and curses a drought into existence in the presence of Ahab. Thus prophet and king are paired against each other as enemies (note Ahab's initial comment to Elijah in 21:20: "Have you found me, O my enemy?"), who embody two different forms of power. The king represents the organized, hierarchical, and centralized power of the state, while the prophet is a charismatic, volatile, and unpredictable voice of protest. The story in I Kings 21, and indeed the whole of I and II Kings is written by someone who favors the voice of prophetic protest. Prophets, after all, tend to be the heroes throughout this history. Nevertheless, the contrast is not absolute. All kings are not evil and all prophets are not good. Evaluation of both must take place on a case by case basis, and the criteria must be how they use or abuse the power that is characteristic of their position.

Structure. The story of Naboth's vineyard extends beyond v. 21a to include all of I Kings 21. The chapter has separate, but interrelated parts. Verses 1-16 are a story about Ahab, Jezebel, and Naboth, which tells how Ahab requested Naboth's vineyard (v. 2), was denied it by the owner (v. 3), pouted (v. 4), and then how Jezebel acquired it for the king by killing Naboth (vv. 5-16). Verses 17-29 are a story about Ahab, Elijah, and God. In this story Elijah is sent to Ahab to deliver two divine oracles (vv. 16-17), which leads to an exchange between Elijah and Ahab (vv. 18-24), and concludes with a final exchange between Ahab and God (vv. 27-29). The two stories are interrelated around the issue of Naboth's vineyard, yet they move in somewhat different directions to explore the danger of different kinds of power.

Significance. Verses 1-16 explore how dangerous a king can be in exploiting power. The opening scene is an exchange between Ahab and Naboth in vv. 1-4. The reference to a palace adjacent to someone else's vineyard in v. 1 sets the stage for a conflict concerning power. Ahab has had such a long history of being interpreted as the enemy of Elijah that it is difficult to interpret any of his actions as positive. And, indeed, he is not a hero in I Kings 21. But his opening speech to Naboth is not exactly an instance of blatant exploitation. He requests in v. 2 to purchase the vineyard from Naboth in exchange for either another vineyard or money. Naboth responds theologically to Ahab's request in v. 3 by citing inheritance law (see Leviticus 25). The owner of the land is ultimately God, who has distributed it to Israel as a portion of their salvation, and thus Naboth does not believe that he has the right to sell what God has given him through his ancestors. The repetition of Naboth's response in v. 4 suggests that Ahab not only understood the theological argument of Naboth, but also was in agreement with it. Nevertheless he pouts because he did not get what he wanted (v. 4).

The second scene is an exchange between Ahab and Jezebel in vv. 5-7. Ahab is pouting and Jezebel inquires as to the reason (v. 5), to which Ahab responds with a partial truth in v. 6. He recounts accurately how he offered Naboth both another vineyard or money for his property, but he does not recount the reason for Naboth's rejection of the offer. He simply states that Naboth refused to sell him the property, without recounting the theological reasons for it. This partial truth complicates the story, for Jezebel now interprets the conflict as being purely between king and subject, and when framed this way, she is clear: Ahab is the king, he can have any vineyard he chooses. Whether the theological reason of divine inheritance would have had any effect on Jezebel is doubtful, but it is noteworthy that this aspect of the discussion is denied her by the pouting Ahab.

The third scene in vv. 8-14 concerns Jezebel, and it recounts how she orchestrated the murder of Naboth. The irony here is that she uses theological arguments to kill him, by accusing the man of cursing God (and king).

The final scene in vv. 15-16 turns the focus back to Ahab, who is pictured walking down to Naboth's vineyard in order to lay claim on it. This is a complex story that presents gradations of evil whose net effect is murder of a human and theft from God. The gradations of evil trace how the organized and bureaucratic power of a king can be dangerous. What began with a pouting king (Ahab), led to the telling of half truths (Ahab), to the manipulation of others lower in the hierarchical structure (elders and scoundrels), to the perversion of religion and piety for political gain (accusation of cursing God), and finally to the plotting and execution of murder (Jezebel) and theft from God (vineyard). In the story of Naboth we see how a certain kind of power has been let loose with the result that it has polluted an entire community. Guilt in this case is systemic, for it incorporates the whole.

Verses 17-29 explore the charismatic power of the prophet. In the first scene this power is positive, for it allows God to break through the polluted system of the monarch. Divine oracles predominate in vv. 17-19. We read that the "word of the LORD came to Elijah" (v. 17) and that Elijah was given two specific oracles in v. 19 ("Thus says the LORD"): the first is to state the sin to Ahab (murder and theft) and the second is to proclaim the punishment (a cursed death). The second scene raises questions about Elijah. There are no divine oracles in this exchange between prophet and king, and instead, we have two forms of power in conflict. The king labels Elijah as enemy, to which the prophet responds by referring to himself in the first person: "I have found you. Because you have sold yourself to do what is evil in the sight of the LORD." So far this speech sounds just fine, because the prophet still seems to be speaking for God. But note how the first person discourse continues in vv. 21-24 without any messenger formulas to qualify the speech as a divine discourse. Elijah states to Ahab: "I will bring disaster on you; I will consume you," and "I will make your house like the house of Jeroboam." This "I" in Elijah's speech is no longer God speaking but the prophet speaking for himself, and it raises the suspicion that the prophet is now guilty of taking his own charismatic power to a vindictive level—a holier-than-thou exercise in fanaticism, which appears to cherish the bloodbath that awaits the king. Such a suspicion finds support in the closing verses of the chapter where God does clearly reenter the narrative in vv. 28-29, and in contrast to the prophet's vindictive threats, forgives a repentant Ahab.

I Kings 21 provides the preacher with a wide range of reflection on the dangers of two types of power. One is the power of systems that are represented by kings and governments and the other is the power of charisma that is represented by prophets. The overarching message of I Kings 21 is a criticism of the king, but the construction of the story forces us out of a too easily stereotyped answer on how we must exercise power. The only real hero in this story is Naboth, who realized that any power or security that he possessed was a gift from God, which he could not afford to sell at any price and it cost him his life. No other character in the narrative shares this insight to the degree of Naboth.

The Response: *Psalm 5:1-8*

A Prayer of Naboth

Setting. Psalm 5 is categorized as an individual lament. The setting is of someone who has been falsely accused and has found sanctuary from the threat of danger in the Temple.

Structure. Psalm 5:1-8 separates into three parts. Verses 1-3 are an appeal to God, who is identified as king. Verses 4-7 expresses confidence that evil will not endure (vv. 4-6) and that the psalmist will enter the sanctuary (v. 7). Verse 8 expresses the petition of the psalmist for divine leading.

Significance. As a response to I Kings 21 the words of the psalm can only be those of Naboth. He was the one falsely accused. Once framed in this way the words of the psalm take on a certain poignancy as commentary on the Old Testament lesson, especially the psalmist's claim that the "LORD abhors the bloodthirsty (Elijah?) and deceitful (Ahab?)."

New Testament Texts

The epistle reading is a bold declaration, indeed a warning, calling for those who have trusted God's work in Jesus Christ for their salvation to remain steadfast in their confidence of the all-sufficient nature of God's grace. The Gospel lesson presents a complex of themes, but prominent among them are Jesus' power and authority to forgive and heal, coupled with the recognition that those who truly experience God's grace live altered lives characterized by generosity, even extravagant generosity compatible with God's extravagant grace.

The Epistle: *Galatians 2:15-21*

The Necessity of Full Faith in Christ

Setting. Paul's letter to the Galatians is one of his so-called major writings. The problem he faces is that the believers in the churches in Galatia have come under the influence of a group of outsiders (other early Christian missionaries). The message of the preachers who came to Galatia after Paul had established congregations in that region was different from the basic gospel Paul had preached. These later preachers declare the saving work of God in Christ, and they insist that God's work through Christ means that Gentiles who become Christians are obligated to observe critical portions of Jewish law—specifically: circumcision, certain calendar events, and dietary restrictions. Paul's letter is a complex argument designed to stop the Galatians from becoming law-observant, for he understands that to embrace the law is to deny the complete sufficiency of God's work for salvation in Jesus Christ.

Specifically, Galatians 2:15-21 is the conclusion of a larger report in 2:11-21 (or 2:1-21). Preceding our text, Paul has reported conflicts over insistence that Gentile Christians observe the law; he recalls especially an incident in Antioch when he vehemently reprimanded Cephas before the assembly of believers. Paul reports part of his remarks on that occasion. Then, and now in relation to the Galatians, Paul declares that an attempt to base one's relationship to God on one's observance of the law is a denial of the reality of the relationship between God and humanity established by God and based in faith in Jesus Christ.

Structure. The shifts in vv. 15-17 to the first person plural ("we") from the second person singular ("you") in v. 14, and, in turn, to the first person singular ("I") in vv. 18-21 probably mark out the contours of Paul's rhetoric. Moving from the report in v. 14, the verses of our reading first issue a summary statement (2:15-17) and, then, apply and expound Paul's position (2:18-21). Thus, the pattern demonstrated by the passage that may inform preaching is declaration, application, and explication.

Significance. This passage is a notoriously difficult one for interpreters of Galatians, and the exact sense of vv. 15 and 17 are highly debated. Verse 15 may be read in at least two ways, and it has been—even by single interpreters. In 1519 Martin Luther gave lectures on Galatians and argued that 2:15 began, "We are sinners of Jewish, not Gentile origin. . . . " But in 1531 he held that the verse began by saying, "We are Jews by nature and not Gentile sinners. . . . " The problem is that the verb is absent from the Greek, so that in any translation a form of "to be" must be supplied (in context, "are"); the debate is where to place the word *are*.

A decision relates to the interpretation of the word *sinners.* Does *sinners* name (a) those set against or outside God's will or (b) those who simply do not keep the law, in detail or at all. Interpreters are sharply divided on which sense *sinners* carries both here and in v. 17. Yet, careful study of the term *sinners* outside Galatians finds that Paul consistently employed the word to name those set against God. Because the word is rare in Paul's letters, however, this observation creates no absolute case that *sinners* must have the same sense in Galatians. But, if a sensible interpretation can be offered that reads this passage in harmony with other uses of *sinners* in Paul's letters, perhaps one should prefer a uniform to a fractured reading of the texts. In other words, there is much to commend Luther's first interpretation over his later understanding and over the translation of the NRSV.

Verse 16 is a clear statement of the unifying convictions of early Jewish Christians: No one is justified from works of the law; rather, those who are justified are justified (literally!) "through the faith of Jesus Christ." Paul declares that what God achieved in Jesus Christ, not what believers accomplish by the practice of piety, sets humanity right with God. Paul repeats this point in two ways in v. 16. Notice the juxtapositions: works versus faith; law versus Jesus Christ. Especially in the context of Galatians we should be careful not to turn faith into the one essential work that brings salvation. Paul is not so much arguing against pious living as he is against the idea that pious living keeps us in God's good graces. Indeed, Paul insists here that God's grace keeps us in God's good graces (v. 17). Christians are sinners, saved and sustained by grace!

Paul continues (vv. 18-21) to meditate on grace by exposing the false notion that the practice of piety somehow gives the practitioners a leg up on the rest of humanity when it comes to God's favor. Since all humans are sinners (Jews and Gentiles alike), God's work in Christ is the hope of all humankind. But Paul goes on to warn that a false understanding of pious practice can even be dangerous. To assume that we can or must do something to enable God's saving work in Jesus Christ is to deny the power of God the creator to justify a broken and sinful creation. Paul's point is crystal clear in v. 21. In these verses and throughout this letter Paul rejects the idea that those "in Christ" are obliged to act in pursuit of their justification, for according to the apostle those "in Christ" are justified by God and are being justified by God alone. Those who live "in Christ" relate to God in faith and are no longer driven by sin's deception, "seeking to be justified," as are those living in the present evil age (Paul's description in Galatians 1:4 of the world without Christ).

The Gospel: *Luke 7:36–8:3*

The Experience of Grace and the Character of Transformation

Setting. The reading brings together two distinct, actually independent passages, perhaps because of the proximity of grateful women in the stories in 7:36-50 and 8:1-3; but whatever the motive for designating 7:36–8:3 as the lesson for this Sunday, there is too much text offered for coherent preaching. One will do well to select either the first or the second unit in the lesson.

The story of Jesus and the woman of the city in the home of the Pharisee, Simon, is part of a larger section running from 7:1-50, which tells of the beginning of the separation of Jesus from Israel. The report of Jesus and the twelve being accompanied by women, some of whom are named, is the first portion of a section telling of Jesus' calling people through word and mighty deed (8:1-56). Two items merit notice: In dealing with the units of the lesson it is helpful to understand the overarching themes of the larger sections in which the passages are located, and one should resist the popular tendency to identify the woman in the first story with Mary Magdalene who is named in the second.

Structure. Luke 7:36-50 is regarded as special Lukan material by most commentators—that is, a tradition without real parallel in the other Gospels. The story, however, reminds one of the anointing of Jesus immediately prior to his Passion in Mark 14:3-9, and remarkably, Luke does not include that account in his version of the Passion. Moreover, in 7:36-50 Jesus tells a story that reminds Luke's reader of the parable of the two debtors in Matthew 18:23-35 (special Matthean material) and of several controversy-stories concerned with Jesus' authority to forgive sins (Matthew 12:9-14; Mark 3:1-6; Luke 6:6-11; 14:1-6). Thus, Luke 7:36-50 is a complex account concerned with Jesus' authority, gratitude as the evidence of the experience of grace, and forgiveness which means living an appropriately altered life.

In turn, the second portion of our lesson (8:1-3) tells of the women who accompanied and supported Jesus and the twelve. Initially one learns that these women had experienced healing in the context of Jesus' ministry. Again, this brief narrative notice, which serves as a transition into the next segment of Luke's account, informs the reader that the experience of grace evoked the response of generous loyalty. On the basis of this theme one may tie 7:36-50 and 8:1-3 together, although they are independent traditions.

Significance. The story of Jesus at table in the home of Simon the Pharisee shows us Jesus and a representative of the recognized exemplars of traditional piety in dialogue. Jesus was not a purely traditional religious leader, but he was also not a simple iconoclast. Moreover, Luke recalls that the Pharisees were not completely hostile to Jesus; they engaged in conversation and debate with him, although at times his words and deeds seemed scandalous. (Even in the world today, religious leaders worry privately and publicly that Jesus often seems so "liberal.")

As Jesus dined with Simon, the woman of the city—a prostitute—came among the banquet guests. Her exceptional behavior demonstrated the overwhelming gratitude for grace of a truly forgiven sinner. But her actions provoked pious reservations on the part of the more proper guests. The story forms a commentary on who really experiences God's grace. Simply put, those whose lives show uncommon generosity in relation to God's work are those who demonstrate the power of grace at work in their lives. Strikingly, Jesus tells a strange truth: Pious person (and, perhaps, impious ones) with little awareness of their sinfulness are least capable of experiencing grace and leading radically altered lives; whereas when those who recognize their sinfulness encounter God's grace in Jesus Christ they experience a liberation that transforms their existence.

The reservation of the properly pious in this account forms that group's own condemnation: They live the form of religion without the passion of the experience of God in their lives. Yet, one should see in this story that Jesus comes to the confidently pious and the sinful alike, and ultimately he wills and acts to bring God's forgiveness to bear on their lives.

In the note about the women who followed and provided for Jesus and the twelve, one finds still another illustration of the reality of grace resulting in a life of generosity on the part of those who are touched by grace. In his openness Jesus ministered to and incorporated the marginal members of his society into God's gracious work. Liberation was not, however, merely accepted or enjoyed by the women Jesus healed; rather, freed from one form of oppression, these women were freed for service and discipleship—despite the second-class citizenship they were afforded by the world in which they lived. Grace grants us freedom to do God's will whatever the structures of the world around us.

Proper 6: The Celebration

Today's lesson from Luke may be used to illustrate the theological content of the lesson from Galatians. It may also serve as an antidote to that antinomianism that is sometimes tortured out of Paul's statements about being free from the law. Notice that the woman who anointed Jesus practically overwhelmed him with pious actions, and rather than reproving her, Jesus pointed out to his host that he had neglected to perform any of those actions. The point is that the pious and generous actions of the woman in the Gospel lesson are subsequent to and in response to the saving presence of Christ. Indeed, even though the assurance of pardon came after the anointing, there is no indication that it was bestowed as a reward for services rendered. The woman's act of devotion was a result of her perception of Christ's, not Simon's, hospitality, and her grief over the disparity between her sinfulness and his gracious acceptance.

The banquet setting of the Gospel lesson suggests that the Lord's Supper might be celebrated today. An act of confession and pardon should certainly be a part of the liturgy. How often has the Church acted the role of Simon at the Lord's Supper with its greater concern for fencing the table and identifying those who are not deemed to be worthy guests than for exercising hospitality and proclaiming how great a debt all have been forgiven! At communion, Brian Wren's hymn, "I Come with Joy to Meet My Lord," with its reference to "his life laid down for me" will unite the image of the meal with the atonement theology of the epistle reading. Many popular gospel hymns are rich with atonement images. They would be easy to use during the reception of communion because many of the congregation will be able to sing them without the aid of hymnals.

Preachers who wish to work out of the Old Testament reading but would like to have a more thematic connection with the New Testament might consider using Luke 20:9-19, the story of the wicked tenants, as the Gospel reading. It does not appear elsewhere in the lectionary and would maintain the use of Luke as the primary Gospel for Year C. Here the tenants are to be seen in the role of Ahab, those who are not content with what has been entrusted to them but are covetous for more, and Naboth stands in parallel to the son who is killed for the inheritance. A sensitive use of the two stories in tandem will consider the consequences of ignoring the claims of God to the sovereign place in life and claiming more for ourselves than we have any right to. The preacher should remember that the primary text in this case is I Kings, not Luke, and avoid the temptation to explicate both stories in full.

Regardless of which text is used today, an appropriate sermon hymn is "My God, I Love Thee" ("I Love Thee, Lord" in some versions): *The Hymnal 1982* (Episcopal), no. 682; *Hymnal: A Worship Book* (Church of the Brethren and Mennonite), no. 605; *The United Methodist Hymnal,* no. 470.

June 12 is Philippine Independence Day. That country, its people, and churches may be remembered in the intercessions.

Proper Seven
Sunday Between June
19 and 25 Inclusive
(If After Trinity Sunday)

Old Testament Texts

I Kings 19:1-15a is the account of Elijah's flight from Israel to Mount Horeb where he receives a revelation at the mountain. Psalms 42–43 combine to form a lament.

The Lesson: *I Kings 19:1-15*a

Hearing God in the Sounds of Silence

Setting. Although the lesson for last week is out of sequence with the Old Testament text for this week, it does, nevertheless, provide important background for interpreting I Kings 19. Last week we saw how Elijah and Ahab were pitted against each other as enemies and how Ahab's wife Jezebel was able to take on a strong role in Ahab's affairs. All of these dimensions play a role in I Kings 19. In its present context this chapter is meant to follow from the confrontation between Elijah and the four hundred prophets of Baal in I Kings 18, who were killed by Elijah. This action provides transition to I Kings 19, for Ahab recounts the massacre to Jezebel (v. 1), who wastes no time informing Elijah that he will quickly join the four hundred prophets of Baal. The story that follows is paradoxical, because this seemingly Rambo-like prophet, who, up to this point has feared neither king nor opposing prophets, suddenly loses all courage and flees south for his life.

Structure. The setting and events of the story are quickly put into place in vv. 1-3. Ahab recounts the massacre of the prophets to Jezebel (v. 1), she finds Elijah someplace in the northern kingdom of Israel and threatens to kill him (v. 2), and, before we even have time

42

to comprehend this sequence of events, the prophet is already in Beersheba, a city in southern Judah (v. 3). Clearly this rapid sequence of events was meant to get the prophet into the southern wilderness, which will be the location for the remainder of the narrative. A series of epiphanies by an angel in vv. 4-8 structure the narrative in such a way that Elijah eventually ends up at Mount Horeb, which becomes the location for theophany in vv. 9-15 (or better through v. 18).

Significance. Last week we noted how there was some ambiguity concerning the quality of Elijah's charismatic and prophetic power. He certainly speaks for God, but he does not hesitate to add his own point of view. The same ambiguity surrounds his introduction in I Kings 17. There is no question from the outset that he is powerful, but upon first appearance he seems to be a "loose gun." The opening verse of chapter 17 presents the central uncertainty about Elijah, when he comes out of no place, appears before Ahab, and quite literally curses a drought into existence: "As the LORD lives," which might be paraphrased, "By God, there is going to be a drought!" And, indeed, there is one by v. 2! He certainly has power, but he is also scary because his opening curse is not kosher language for a Hebrew prophet. We would haved expected some form of a messenger formula to authenticate the oracle from Elijah, like, "Thus says the Lord." But no such formula appears, and without any past history to evaluate this "prophet," we are forced to read on apprehensively. The reader's potential uncertainty is not shared by the prophet. In fact it is Elijah's opening fearlessness and self-confidence of being God's spokesperson regardless of commission that has propelled the events leading up to I Kings 19: the drought (I Kings 17) led to a confrontation between Elijah and the prophets of Baal (I Kings 18), prompting Jezebel's threat and Elijah's flight (I Kings 19). By the time the reader reaches I Kings 19, enough episodes have taken place to make Elijah's sudden loss of courage paradoxical, at the very least. This paradox is underscored even further by the writers, when the prophet is not only pictured as fleeing for his life but also as requesting death in v. 4. This is not the very self-confident drought-inducing character that burst onto the scene in I Kings 17:1.

Elijah's loss of confidence and death wish in the setting of the southern wilderness set the stage for a series of epiphanies that address the problem of charismatic power which is represented by the prophet. As soon as the prophet reaches a point of hopelessness in v. 4, God enters the story as the primary character through a sequence of three epiphanies, which provide a framework for Elijah's journey to Mount Horeb: Twice an angel comes to Elijah to feed him and to direct him on a forty-day trip to Mount Horeb (vv. 5-6, 7-8), which results in a third epiphany when God asks him what he is doing at Mount Horeb (vv. 9-10 and 13*b*-14). These epiphany stories give way to a more detailed account of theophany on Mount Horeb in vv. 11-13*a*, which is the central point of the text. The account of theophany on Mount Horeb includes all of the classical elements that Elijah would expect in a revelation from God: a powerful wind, an earthquake, and fire. Yet God is in none of them. Finally there is the sound of silence, which has no tradition in ancient Israel for being a channel of divine appearance. Yet God is in it. After Elijah recognizes God in the sound of silence, the story starts anew, this time with a series of explicit divine commissions as opposed to Elijah's earlier self-proclaimed curse.

Two themes are worthy of reflection in preaching this text. The first is the central role of reversal throughout the narrative both in the development of character and in the communication of God. Elijah is transformed from an overly confident prophetic figure to a potentially suicidal individual, while divine revelation is absent in the expected occurrences of wind, fire, and earthquake only to appear in the still small voice. When these two reversals are interpreted within the structure of the narrative, they raise the question concerning which portrait of Elijah is heroic.

The second theme follows from the first—namely, the role of charismatic power in this text. Individual charisma and the power of singular personalities have taken center stage as the ideal model of leadership in much of the Protestant church today. Such models accentuate strong individuals who are able to shape entire communities through the force of their will. Such power is certainly important in the Old Testament, and it is sometimes idealized in prophetic figures like Elijah. But it is also seen to be a dangerous force among the people of God. Legends surrounding the prophet Elijah are one of the places where both the strengths and weaknesses of such charisma are explored. Elijah is certainly powerful in the way that he is presented throughout the story, but biblical writers do not overly embrace him. His character is sketched out as being too individualistic and, consequently, on the fringes of control. He certainly is against the worship of Baal, which is clearly good, but what is the point of the drought? Such doubts about his character are introduced in the opening verse of I Kings 17, and they linger into I Kings 19, until the prophet internalizes them himself in his flight from Jezebel and his death wish in the wilderness. Interestingly, it is at this point that biblical writers weave in Elijah's central experience of theophany, in which he perceives God in silence. Such perception results in a series of commissions and in the insight that, indeed, the prophet was never alone but part of a group of seven thousand that remained loyal to God.

The Response: *Psalms 42–43*

A Lament

Setting. Psalms 42–43 appear to form one unit. The strongest evidence for this conclusion is the repetition of the refrain in 42:5, 11 and 43:5: "Why are you cast down, O my soul, and why are you disquieted within me? Hope in God; for I shall again praise him, my help and my God." The words of the refrain help in categorizing Psalms 42–43 as a lament.

Structure. The refrain breaks up the structure of Psalms 42–43 so that it forms three parts, and it provides the conclusion to each section. Psalm 42:1-5 describes the psalmist's situation of despair, which is intensified in 42:6-11 and continued through 43:1-5.

Significance. The genre of lament provides important commentary on the Elijah story, since his insight into the power of God came only after he had reached a situation of lamentation in the wilderness. Once this connection is made, the contrasts within the psalm of past strength (v. 4) and present weakness (v. 9) provide still further reflection on the Old Testament lesson. The refrain is crucial in worship, however, because it provides insight into the character of God who is a source of hope even when present experience would deny it.

New Testament Texts

The epistle reading presents a portion of Paul's argument against the Galatians' inclination toward observance of the law. Paul informs the Galatians that a move from the current life of faith in Christ to a life of observing minute laws is a move from the present and God's future into the past, a past that God has labored in Christ to overcome. The Gospel lesson tells the story of one of the best-known incidents in the ministry of Jesus, the healing of a man possessed by a legion of demons. Luke's telling of the story contrasts points of view of the characters in the story on Jesus and registers a profound christological point.

The Epistle: *Galatians 3:23-29*

The End of the Law and the Coming of Faith

Setting. Galatians 3:1–6:10 contains a series of arguments against the tendency of the Galatians to become observant of the law. Paul's tactics are creative. He argues logically and exegetically, both by analogy and through allegory to make his point and to win his case. At the outset of chapter 3, Paul confronts the Galatians with the inappropriateness of their concern with the law; then, he takes up the story of Abraham (and Christ) to argue that the law is irrelevant for the Galatians, and Paul continues throughout the course of chapter 3 to clarify the true nature of the law. This initial line of reflection comes to a climax in the verses of our reading.

Structure. The framework of Paul's reasoning in these verses is temporal. He contrasts "then" (before faith came) with "now" (Christ came). Having contrasted the times, he continues to create contrasts by juxtaposing the idea of being under the law over against the ideas of being justified by faith and not being under a custodian. Thus, Paul shows the necessity of a choice between "law" and "faith"; and he declares the irrelevance of the law for Christians (vv. 23-25).

In the following verses Paul explicates his position (vv. 26-28). He informs the Galatians that they are children of God through faith in Christ Jesus. The concrete evidence of this spiritual reality is given in the baptism of the Galatians—into Christ. Together in Christ, believers are united, so that old distinctions from the previous time (then) are gone. Thus, the hallmark of Judaism, observance of the law, is extinct. From this point, in v. 29 Paul concludes his reasoning in this section with a declaration concerning the Galatians' inheritance of the benefits of the promise to Abraham.

Significance. Two features of these verses make them challenging for preaching. First, the real concern of the Galatians to become law-observant is likely without parallel today. Very few Gentile Christians are eager to become like Hasidic Jews. Yet congregations are still tempted toward all kinds of legalisms, which provide a sense of security. Many ask innocently, "How am I to be a Christian? Tell me the rules!" Second, Paul's thinking here about Christ is both real and symbolic. The historical dimension of Paul's thought is fairly straightforward, but the symbolic dimension of Paul's reflection is difficult for twentieth-century persons. Paul casts Christ as the cosmic man to whom all Christians are called to conform. Today, such thinking will seem abstract, but it is not; yet it may be necessary to restate Paul's point this way: Through faith we have a relationship to Christ, and in that relationship we are called to become ever more like our Lord. Christ's reality is the standard toward which God is calling our lives.

Galatians 3:28 is one of the best-known lines in Pauline literature. This elegant statement of Christian unity takes on even greater force as we view it in the context of Paul's reasoning in Galatians. Effectively, the move of the Galatians to observe the law is a move to act distinctively so that they can distinguish themselves from others. Paul declares that God's work in Jesus Christ eliminates such old distinctions, for being in Christ is itself that which distinguishes persons of faith. The Galatians are in danger of attempting to recreate the very distinctions that separate portions of humanity from one another, so that they deny and defy the unifying and saving work of God.

Above all, however, Paul declares the good news that "faith has come." Remarkably, Paul contends that faith came into the world, establishing the reality of a new relationship between God and humanity, in the very person and faithfulness of Jesus Christ. The law and faith are at odds when people turn to the law with the expectation that law-observance will do for them what God in Christ has already done.

Paul understands that God's saving work eliminates ethnic, social, and sexual divisions. He does not blindly deny these realities; rather he proclaims that they are undone! Old barriers have been broken down as God through Christ calls humans beyond their particularities to a new Christ-formed existence that is characterized by mutual commitment to Christ, not by particular commitments that set one person or group against another.

The Gospel: *Luke 8:26-39*

Jesus: Master over Demons and Savior of Humanity

Setting. In relation to the Gospel lesson for last Sunday we noted that Luke 8 treats the theme of Jesus' calling persons through words and mighty deeds. The story of the Gerasene demoniac, however, is more the story of a commission than a call. Here we find Jesus making the single journey into Gentile territory that Luke recounts. As Jesus turns to the people of Israel with teaching and healing, we see his work in relation to a Gentile in a manner that anticipates the full, unhindered proclamation of the Gospel to the Gentiles—the story which Luke tells in Acts.

Structure. This lesson illustrates the care with which Luke crafted his version of the story of Jesus' ministry. In comparison with the versions of this narrative in Matthew 8:28-34 and Mark 5:1-20, one finds that Luke's account is much closer to Mark's than Matthew's; but, even so, Luke seems to give the story his own distinct touches. In style and structure, Luke offers a polished, logically ordered report with sensible narrative development. Comparison of the verses of this lesson with Mark's account will highlight Luke's emphases.

At its heart, this account is a miracle story. One observes the basic elements of a standard ancient account: problem, action, resolution or confirmation of solution. Yet Luke offers much detail in this story that is not typical of stock miracle accounts, and the crucial epilogue to this story registers important theological themes.

Significance. The rich details in this account reveal Luke's concern to show the degree of the problem Jesus encountered as he faced the man from the Gerasene territory. Among the several items used to inform the reader of the Gospel about the identity of this man is the name "Legion." It is a borrowed word from Latin that designates a body of soldiers numbering between four and six thousand. Whereas one demon is enough to wreck a human's life, this poor man is beset by thousands. But, as is often the case, modern readers who do not live with a daily sense of the reality of demons may have trouble with this account. A major effort to rehabilitate belief in literal demons will stray from the central concerns of the text and will not result in much "good news" being proclaimed. Yet, on the other hand, a well-meant effort to explain the demons away— for example, the psychological contention that the man was suffering from the schizophrenia of multiple personalities—also misses the force of the story. The demons in this account represent evil; indeed, they are enormous evil itself. Thus, we hear of Jesus' facing the assembled forces of evil, of his actions in relation to evil, and of the consequences. Modern readers may not think much about demons, but anyone who reads the newspaper has to take the reality of evil seriously. Preachers' minds will be challenged as they seek to retell this story in relation to the everyday life that members of their congregations face, but the reality of evil and the reality of Christ are the given elements of this text that demand translation.

As Jesus arrives on the shore of the territory of the Gerasenes one is reminded of his presence in our lives. In this story he is present in the life of the demoniac, present in the lives of the townspeople, and even present in the lives of the demons! For the purposes of this story the disciples are merely onlookers—onlookers from afar. Finding ways to speak of the presence or the perception of the presence of Christ in our lives may provide entry into the preaching of this text.

Standing before the demoniac, Jesus is recognized for who he is—if not by the man at least by the hoard of demons who have beset him. Here is a first hint of Luke's passionate message: Jesus comes into the context of human life as the very Son of God; and, as such, he comes with awesome power. Jesus' presence and power seem to create fear on the part of the demons, and later in the story his person and work clearly cause fear on the part of the people who come out to witness the results of Jesus' dramatic healing of the demon-possessed man.

Notice that the various characters in the story make requests of the authoritative Son of God. First, the demons ask not to be returned to the abyss. Strangely, their request seems to be granted. They go into the pigs (why are there so many pigs so close to kosher Jewish territory?) and, although they plunge the pigs into the sea, they are not in the abyss. Second, the demoniac who is healed asks to follow Jesus. His request is denied. Gentiles are not yet among the followers, but this man foreshadows the future and reveals the outcome of the work of Christ. Third, the people of the region ask Jesus to leave. Again, the request is granted. Jesus goes away, proving that some sad human bidings are given heed by the divine. The implications of these petitions and responses is rich.

Finally, the exchange between Jesus and the man whom he has healed is the heart of the story. The man asks to follow Jesus, but Jesus instructs him to go and tell all that God had done for him. The man goes, and he tells all that Jesus had done. Luke is no sloppy writer. The point is clear: What God does God does through Jesus, God's son. In the person and work of Jesus God confronts and defeats evil so that we humans are set free to live the lives God intends for us to experience—lives that "make known" the saving love of God.

Proper 7: The Celebration

Today's Old Testament lesson is the source for the concluding lines of John Greenleaf Whittier's hymn, "Dear Lord and Father of Mankind." Ironically, because of the complexity of the English language and the way meanings are heard differently from generation to generation, most congregations, when they sing:

> Breathe through the heats of our desire
> thy coolness and thy balm;
> let sense be dumb, let flesh retire;
> speak through the earthquake, wind, and fire,
> O still, small voice of calm

hear exactly the opposite of what Whittier (and the author of I Kings) intended. When the poet says, "speak through the earthquake, wind, and fire," he does not mean through in the sense of an agent or "by means of." It is a use of *through* that means to work through something without being overwhelmed by it, as in, "I heard the whisper through the howling of the wind," which is to say that the howling did not provide an obstacle to the whispered message. The same use is employed earlier in the stanza, "Breathe through the heats of our desire," but there it seems to be more properly understood since "coolness and balm" are obviously in contrast to heat. "Through" in this stanza means "in spite of."

The hymn as we know it from our hymnals is part of a larger work, "The Brewing of Soma," which the Quaker Whittier wrote as a protest against the sensual excesses of revivalism. He compared the evangelistic techniques he saw being used around him to the use of strong drink in other cultures to induce religious ecstasy.

> In sensual transports wild as vain
> We brew in many a Christian fane [temple]
> The heathen Soma still.

"Dear Lord and Father of Mankind" is composed of the last part of the poem where he contrasts an attitude of trustful waiting upon God with our feverish ways of seeking religious experience.

The importance of silence in worship may consequently be stressed today, not only in the sermon (a non-silent event, after all), but in the order of service itself. We westernized Christians tend not to handle silence very well. "Silent Meditation," when it appears in the bulletin, is usually accompanied by music, so genuine silence is avoided even in worship.

> If our life is poured out in useless words, we will never hear anything, will never become anything, and in the end, because we have said everything before we had anything to say we shall be left speechless at the moment of our greatest decision. (Thomas Merton, *Thoughts in Solitude* [New York: Dell, 1961], pp. 114-15)

Because of its strangeness in our culture, congregations will probably require some help learning to use silence in their worship. Silence may need to be directed so that people will know what to do with it and understand its function at appropriate places in the liturgy. A time of silence, for example, may be the form of response to a lesson, and the liturgist may introduce it by saying, "Let us now spend some time in silence as we allow the noises of our lives to die away and the still, small voice to speak." Silence may also be used between the time that the congregation is invited to pray and the actual prayer is said. This allows for the whole assembly to focus on the task at hand. In a printed bulletin, the form may look like this:

> The Lord be with you.
> **And also with you.**
> Let us pray. [a brief silence is kept] Almighty God, . . .

For those churches that try to schedule baptisms in relation to the appointed lessons, the epistle and the Gospel readings provide some fascinating images to give insight into the meaning of the rite. Paul talks about being clothed with Christ in baptism. This may have some reference to the new clothes put on by the baptizands after coming up out of the water, a sign that they are a new creation and their identity is given to them by their incorporation into Christ, no matter how they may be classified or stigmatized in the world. The preacher might wish to use Genesis 3 in this case as the Old Testament lesson, for there sin is portrayed as making possible the distinctions we use to differentiate among ourselves and to oppress one another, and the attempts that are made at clothing are finally ineffectual. In Luke, water is the vehicle used to destroy the forces of evil that invade our lives and tyrannize over us.

The lessons suggest the following concerns for intercessions: those who are being persecuted, those who feel alienated from God and all alone, those who are preparing for baptism, victims of discrimination, those possessed by evil thoughts and inclinations. Silence may also be used after each individual invitation to prayer.

Proper Eight
Sunday Between
June 26 and July 2
Inclusive

Old Testament Texts

Second Kings 2:1-2, 6-14 is the account of Elijah being carried off into heaven. Psalm 77:1-2, 11-20 is a hymn that celebrates the past salvific acts of God.

The Lesson: *II Kings 2:1-2, 6-14*

Ascension and the Passing On of the Mantle

Setting. II Kings 2 links the prophetic careers of Elijah and Elisha. The stories of Elijah include I Kings 17–19, 21, and II Kings 1–2. Elisha is first mentioned in I Kings 19:19-21 as a disciple of Elijah, and he returns in the same role in the lectionary text for this Sunday. Stories about Elisha become central from the end of II Kings 2 through the beginning of II Kings 9, and his death is reported in II Kings 13:14-21. The sketch of the distribution of stories about Elijah and Elisha illustrates how there are really two distinct cycles of tradition about each prophet, and that they have now been woven into a larger story by means of the motif of succession. Succession, therefore, will provide a central point for interpreting II Kings 2:1-12.

Structure. Some form of interrelationship has been established between II Kings 1 and 2. Second Kings 1 is a story about Elijah denouncing King Ahaziah, who has injured himself and is seeking divine counsel from the foreign god Baalzebub. Elijah stops the messengers on the way to Baalzebub and predicts the king's death because he did not inquire of the Lord (vv. 1-4). King Ahaziah is upset by the news of his impending death and commands his soldiers to bring Elijah to him (vv. 5-8). The remainder of the chapter consists of three groups of fifty soldiers, who approach Elijah sitting on a mountain. As the first two groups approach Elijah, he summarily calls down divine fire upon them (vv. 9-10, 11-12). The captain of the third group breaks this pattern by requesting that the prophet spare his life, at which time an angel of the Lord tells Elijah to go to King Ahaziah and confirm the announcement of his death (vv. 13-16). The chapter ends with King Ahaziah dying (vv. 17-18).

Second Kings 2 is a story about Elijah's ascension into heaven (v. 1). As in II Kings 2, the chapter separates into a three-part sequence, with the third section departing from the stereotyped pattern of the first two. Twice Elijah commands Elisha to depart from him, once at Bethel and a second time at Jericho. In each case Elisha refuses, prophets tell Elisha that Elijah is about to ascend, and Elisha responds by confirming their insight and by telling them to be silent (vv. 2-3, 4-5). The third instance takes place by the Jordan River (vv. 6-8). The stereotyped pattern begins (Elijah commands Elisha to depart, the latter refuses), but then it ceases when Elijah parts the Jordan River with his mantle in the witness of fifty prophets, so that he and Elisha can cross on dry ground. Clearly there is a relationship between the three-part structure of II Kings 1 and II Kings 2, especially between the fifty prophets that witness the crossing and the fifty soldiers that are spared the fire from heaven. The two stories diverge, however, at this point: instead of a king dying in I Kings 1:17-18, I Kings 2:9-12 describes Elijah's ascent into heaven.

Significance. Three themes in II Kings 2:1-12 can be explored for preaching: the relationship of Elijah and Elisha, the Exodus imagery in the parting of the Jordan, and the ascension of Elijah.

First, the relationship of Elijah and Elisha. The setting of the Elijah and Elisha texts illustrates how II Kings 2 is meant to link the two prophets, so that Elisha becomes the successor of Elijah. The boundaries of the lectionary text do not bring this theme to its conclusion, since vv. 13-14 describe how Elisha picked up the mantle of Elijah and then parted the Jordan River. The issue of succession, however, is woven throughout the account of the journey from Bethel through Jericho to the Jordan, and the unwillingness of Elisha to leave Elijah can be probed to explore the issue of how prophetic power is passed on.

Second, the Exodus imagery. The power of Elijah to divide the waters and to cross the Jordan on dry ground points the reader back to God's salvation of Israel at the Red Sea. At least two points are being made with the incorporation of this event that can be developed in preaching. One, the imminent power of God to save (and to judge in II Kings 1) is underscored through the work of the prophet. In the traditions of the Exodus, the power of God to control the waters is a sign of divine presence in this world. The repetition of this event signals, at the very least, that the salvation of God is not once and for all, but ongoing in the life of God's prophets. Two, a relationship between Moses-Joshua and Elijah-Elisha is made by having these four characters divide water. The Exodus imagery, therefore, not only says something about the presence of God in this world, but it also ties back to the first point about succession. All of these characters embody the power of God to save, and this power is capable of being transferred.

Third, the ascension of Elijah. Perhaps the most striking aspect of the story is the ascension of Elijah in the chariot of fire. (Although the parting of the Jordan River is no small feat.) The meaning of this imagery is difficult to determine precisely, but it most likely incorporates aspects of Israel's holy war traditions, which were used to describe the character of God's salvation, especially in the Exodus.

The Response: *Psalm 77:1-2, 11-20*

A Celebration of Tradition

Setting. Psalm 77 is difficult to categorize because it switches mood at its midpoint. What begins as a lament turns into a hymnic celebration of tradition.

Structure. The lectionary has recognized the change of mood in the psalm and focused on the hymnic part by limiting the reading primarily to the second half of the psalm in vv. 11-20. Verses 1-2, however, do retain some of the mood of lamenting. Here it is clear that the voice of the psalmist arises out of a situation of trouble.

Significance. The hymnic section in vv. 11-20 provides the best commentary on the Old Testament lesson. As the interpretation above has noted, the ascent of Elijah picks up many of the central motifs of salvation in the Old Testament, while also adding the spectacular image of the prophet riding off into heaven. Hence the celebration of the past wonders of God in the hymnic response allows the congregation to pull this story of Elijah and Elisha into their present worship, thus providing an occasion for the celebration of tradition. Furthermore, the central place of the Exodus in the hymn (v. 16-19) ties in well to the central motif of II Kings 2.

New Testament Texts

The readings bring together Paul's bold and profound declarations and teachings about the life of Christian freedom with a series of stories from the Gospel according to Luke. Paul writes about and around the theme of freedom, whereas the stories in Luke cohere by portraying Jesus' determination to accomplish God's will and his demand that his disciples share that determination.

The Epistle: *Galatians 5:1, 13-25*

"For Freedom Christ Has Set Us Free"

Setting. Throughout Galatians 3–4 Paul offers further arguments attempting to persuade the Galatians, who are Gentiles, not to become observant of the Jewish law. Paul uses both scripture and the experience of the Galatians as he argues through analogy and allegory to make his case. At 5:1 the apostle sums up the point of his argument, but this verse also forms a bridge to the next portion of the letter. By moving to vv. 13-25 the lectionary suggests skipping the essentially negative and historically specific materials in vv. 2-12; no harm is done to the sense of Paul's statements by this omission.

Verse 13 returns overtly to the "freedom" Paul declared in 5:1 and, then, the lines continue by reasoning about what believers are freed from (the "flesh" and the things of the flesh) and what believers are freed for (the "Spirit" and the things of the Spirit). Paul's train of though runs through v. 26, although the lectionary reading stops one verse short of Paul's own conclusion.

Structure. Verse 1 serves to state Paul's theme, and one should probably understand that this statement sets the focus and tone for the rest of the letter. In turn, the remaining verses of the reading fall into three related sections. Verses 13-15 reflect upon the use of freedom. Then, in vv. 16-24, Paul heightens the contrast between appropriate and inappropriate uses of freedom by contrasting the difference between the flesh and the Spirit and the characteristics of each of these important concepts. Finally, in vv. 25-26 Paul offers a concluding comment and an admonition concerning the Spirit. Paul's logic is suggestive and appropriate for the development of a sermon.

Significance. Paul moves away from the allegory of chapter 4 with a direct statement of his thinking in 5:1. Christians are freed by Christ for freedom. The substance of that freedom, however, is not stated here, but with the more elaborate subsequent statement about the Spirit one gets the idea of the meaning and character of Christian freedom. It is striking to notice that the freedom of Christians comes as the result of Christ's own work in freeing believers; yet, vital Christian freedom requires some effort by those whom Christ frees. In the grace of Christ's freedom, Christians are called to resist the oppression of "slavery"—that is, believers are to avoid involvement with systems of religion that afford a false security that thwarts the sometimes frightening liberation they are given by God's grace at work through Christ. Christians are called to resist turning the dynamic life of grace into the more static piety of rule-book religion. The vigor of Paul's declaration, however, indicates the odd, sad fact that the temptation to feel religiously secure often overpowers the will to be divinely freed.

Paul informs the Galatians that since they are freed, they can use their freedom as an opportunity to focus on themselves or as an opportunity to focus on others. Paul implies that the true test of "religion" is its focus. The summary of the law offered in v. 14 cites Leviticus 19:18, but this could also be a memory of the tradition about Jesus' teaching as recorded in Matthew 22:39. Coupled with this admonition to focus on others is the strange statement in v. 15, which seems to warn against hostile behavior. In this context the statement may be a warning against the practice of comparing one another's religious performances in an effort to establish one's own security.

Consulting a theological dictionary concerning Paul's use of the terms *flesh* and *Spirit* will provide insight into his thought in vv. 16-24. Paul is not lapsing here into Platonic dualism that devalues the material world as it praises the world of spiritual things. Rather, in good Jewish fashion, Paul thinks of two opposing wills or forces that drive humans, one set against God and God's ways (the flesh) and one devoted to God and God's will (the Spirit). Paul understands that the power of the Spirit is the power and work of God's own Spirit within the lives of humans, and he calls for believers to walk "in the Spirit" and not "under the law." To make his point Paul offers lists concerning the flesh and the Spirit. In vv. 19-21 he lists the things of the flesh and warns that these characteristics have no inheritance in the present and coming Kingdom of God. By contrast Paul lists the "fruit of the Spirit" in v. 22. This list is not a compendium of spiritual or charismatic gifts, rather these characteristics are the result of the work of the Spirit and all believers should manifest these things. In particular, the word translated *faithfulness* in this list is the Greek word for "faith." The failure of most translations to render this word accurately obscures Paul's basic thought— that is, that the gracious work of God through the Holy Spirit gives Christian life a distinct character that comes as a gift from God.

The end of the reading comes in proverbial pronouncements. Verse 24 makes an observation that could be paraphrased, "You can judge a tree by the fruit it bears." To this observation, v. 25 adds a call. Again, in paraphrase, one might say, "Since the power of the Spirit set you free, why not trust the power of the Spirit to direct a life of genuine freedom?"

The Gospel: *Luke 9:51-62*

The Journey of Jesus to Do God's Will

Setting. At Luke 9:51 one encounters a major turning point in Luke's account. Here the reader finds that Jesus quite deliberately set out toward Jerusalem. The journey of Jesus and his companions to Jerusalem extends from this first notice through 19:27 when the journey is finally complete. The journey, however, is no simple trip. One of Luke's major concerns throughout Luke and Acts is to communicate both who Jesus is and what his "way" is. One learns much about both concerns as one observes, or better, follows Jesus on the way to Jerusalem. Thus, this journey is part of a journey-motif that is more than a log of Jesus' travels.

A careful reading of Luke's writings finds in Luke's language the beginning of Jesus' "way" as a twelve year old in Jerusalem (Luke 2:41-42), and on that occasion one finds that Jesus was devoted above all to God's interests (2:49). Moreover, the journey or way of Jesus does not end when he goes up to Jerusalem in Luke 19:28; rather, Jesus' way is realized or completed with the events of the Ascension in Acts 1 (see especially vv. 10-11). Jesus' way is a course of living, of faithful service to God's will. As Jesus journeys he establishes a pattern of life for his disciples that places uncompromising demands on them, especially in relation to Jesus' promised, future coming.

Structure. The shape of this lesson is clear. Verse 51 signals a new movement and period in the ministry of Jesus. With that sign of the times given, the account continues and the remaining verses of our lesson recall two sets of events. First, one finds the incident concerning the inhospitable Samaritans (vv. 52-56) with the report of the reactions of certain disciples and, then, of Jesus himself. Second, Luke recalls a series of exchanges between Jesus and three would-be disciples (vv. 57-62). The first story illustrates Jesus' determination, especially in contrast to the failure of others to support his efforts. The second story illustrates the costly nature of following the way of Jesus.

Significance. In highly graphic language, v. 51 recognizes the significance and the purpose of the time of Jesus' journey. The mention of Jesus' being taken up binds together the coming episodes in Jesus' ministry, his Passion, Resurrection, and Ascension. The phrase "set his face" is highly Semitic in character, expressing both direction and determination.

As the narrative continues one learns that Jesus' direction and determination determined the directions he gave to his disciples as he dispatched them to go ahead of him and prepare his journey. As the disciples came to a Samaritan village, the villagers refused to receive Jesus. The hostility was the residue of a centuries-old quarrel between the Samaritans and the Jews. Minor theological differences had produced major conflict and occasions of great violence. Thus, the determination to do God's will that directed Jesus toward Jerusalem made him unacceptable to the Samaritans, for they denied Jerusalem's significance as a place of devotion to God. James and John personify the age-old hate of Jews toward Samaritans as they ask about calling for the destruction of the village. They simply assume God's willingness to judge and destroy these people. The devotion of James and John to Jesus is admirable, but their understanding of God's will regarding the Samaritans is deplorable. Thus, Jesus rebukes them. From Jesus' reaction to the reaction of James and John to the action of the Samaritans, we learn a vital theological lesson. God regards hostility such as that portrayed here to be inappropriate, but human ignorance that produces rejection of God's will does not mean that God wills to destroy such humans. The Samaritans rejected Jesus, but, despite the call of the disciples, Jesus does not reject the Samaritans.

The next story of the series of exchanges between Jesus and those who might be disciples reveals the true nature of discipleship. In the first exchange Jesus tells a volunteer for discipleship about the necessity of self-denial when one lives in full devotion to doing God's will. In the second incident Jesus attempts to recruit a disciple, but the recruit hesitates only to be told by Jesus that disciples are called to have God as their ultimate concern. And, in the third exchange, Jesus again meets a volunteer whose double-mindedness evokes Jesus' stern statement about the impossibility of divided loyalties for disciples. The demands of discipleship determine a devoted life of selfless service in the same way that Jesus lived.

Proper 8: The Celebration

Just as Jesus was the man for others, so those who are baptized in Christ (last week's epistle reading) are expected to use their Christian freedom (this week's epistle reading) in a life of discipleship (this week's Gospel reading). In order to avoid turning the passage from Luke into a new set of legalisms, the events should be understood in light of the whole Gospel. The kind of demands that Jesus makes call for a freedom which we are not able to exercise on our own. The fruits of the Spirit enumerated in Galatians 5:22 make possible a self-effacement in the interest of others.

It should be noted that while the excuses offered in Luke 9:59, 61 sound as though someone else is being put first, in fact the individual making the excuse has his own interests at heart, what Clarence Jordan called a "scat-hole."

> Down south we cut a little square hole in the bottom of the door so the cat can have some way to come and go; and when you say, "Scat," he's got some way to go without you gittin' up and openin' the door for him. This boy wanted him a scat-hole so that if the sailin' got rough, and he had to get out of the situation real quick, he could scat. A lot of folks don't wanna cut loose of everything and jump into this thing. They wanna say, "Well, what if this thing folds up?" (Clarence Jordan and Bill Lane Doulos, *Cotton Patch Parables of Liberation* [Scottdale, Pa.: Herald Press, 1976], p. 114)

The Gospel lesson describes the kind of sacrifice Christ is able to make possible in our lives when we live in the freedom he gives. To chastise the three men in the story is to miss the point, because at that time in the narrative Christ had only begun to blaze the trail himself. We must not forget that the Gospels were written with the knowledge of how the story was going to turn out. The story of the three men is told so that we may evaluate our response to the call of Christ in light of the victory he has won for us. Today's sermon may appropriately deal with the tension in Christian living between discipline and freedom, the freedom that makes true discipline possible because we no longer have to prove anything to ourselves or to God. "Make Me a Captive, Lord" suggests itself as the sermon hymn for today.

The following litany of confession and forgiveness is based on today's New Testament readings.

Let us confess our failures in discipleship.
For the times we have preferred our own comfort
and ignored your call to service:

Lord Christ, forgive.

For placing our material welfare above the demands of love:

Lord Christ, forgive.

For blaming others for our own failure to act:

Lord Christ, forgive.

[silent recollection]

For freedom Christ has set us free. Stand firm, therefore, and through love become slaves of one another, for in Christ Jesus our selfishness has been crucified and our sins have been forgiven. If we live by the Spirit, let us be guided by the Spirit.

Amen.

The sermon hymn, if one of the options for the Old Testament reading is used (see commentary), may be "Forward Through the Ages."

Proper Nine
Sunday Between July 3
and 9 Inclusive

Old Testament Texts

Second Kings 5:1-14 is the story of how Elisha cured the leprosy of Naaman. Psalm 30 is a hymn of thanksgiving for God's gift of healing the psalmist.

The Lesson: *II Kings 5:1-14*

The Healing of Naaman

Setting. The healing of Naaman is one episode in the larger cycle of stories about Elisha the prophet. Elisha is introduced in I Kings 19 as the successor of Elijah and becomes the central figure in a series of stories in II Kings 2–9, before his death is recorded in II Kings 13. Many miracle stories are associated with the character of Elisha. He purifies food and water, miraculously feeds one hundred people, raises children from the dead, and is able to cure disease. Even after his death, contact with his bones prompts a resurrection. The story of Naaman being cured from leprosy fits into this larger cycle of miracle stories.

Structure. The boundaries of the lectionary text are limited to the healing of Naaman. His story actually continues through v. 19 where his return to the prophet and conversion to Yahwism is narrated. Then a story of the swindling of Naaman by Elisha's servant, Gehazi, rounds out the chapter. The lectionary text can be separated into four parts. The problem of the narrative is established in vv. 1-3: Naaman has leprosy. The next two sections, vv. 4-7 and 8-12, narrate two intermediate and unsuccessful attempts by Naaman to resolve his problem, until he is finally cured by Elisha in vv. 13-14.

Significance. Many of the commentaries approach this story around its central dynamic of a problem (leprosy in Naaman) seeking a solution (healing from leprosy). And, indeed, this structure is essential for interpreting the story. There is a certain balance in the telling of the story between characters as the plot unravels toward its solution. In the opening section (vv. 1-3) Naaman is introduced, his problem is stated and a servant girl suggests a solution by mentioning the prophet in Samaria (Elisha) who is able to work miracles. Somewhat surprisingly the King of Aram supports Naaman's trip to Israel and sends a letter of introduction with his commander. The king of Israel presents the first obstacle to this solution in the second section (vv. 4-7) by interpreting Naaman's quest for a cure (and the king's letter) as a political ruse to engage Israel in battle. Naaman himself presents the second obstacle in the third section (vv. 8-12). He is a person of high rank who is accustomed to special treatment. And when the prophet does not even bother to leave his tent to give directions on how he might cure himself (washing in the Jordan River seven times), Naaman is offended. He is rescued from his arrogance by his servants in vv. 13-14 (a parallel to the servant girl in the opening section) and thus is healed. This synopsis underscores how there is art in the telling of the story, but such literary insight still leaves open the question of how to preach this text.

The cure of Naaman is a story about the activity of God beyond the boundaries of Israel. The problem in the story, therefore, is how people go about recognizing the activity of God in unexpected places. The way that this point is carried through the story is by keeping the activity of God in the background. There is no divine revelation or prophetic speech in the narrative. Instead the actions of characters determine the degree to which God enters the story. The Israelite king and Naaman represent the two major obstacles. The most negative character in the story is the king, who cannot conceive of God being active beyond the boundaries of Israel. A request for a miracle from Israel's God, therefore, could not possibly be sincere, and it is interpreted as a ruse for battle. Naaman is a mixed character. Verse 1 introduces the tension that surrounds him. He has leprosy and he has found favor with the Lord. This tension gives rise to three questions. First, why the combination of leprosy and divine favor, since leprosy frequently functions as a sign of divine judgment, as it does at the close of the story with Gehazi? And second, why does God favor Naaman at all? He is not an Israelite. And finally, will Naaman be able to recognize this divine preference?

God lurks in the background, thus leaving all of these questions open. Elisha functions almost as indirectly as God in this story, and, in fact, as the healer he comes to embody divine power in the story. Thus, even though this is an episode in the larger cycle of Elisha stories, the prophet does not take center stage. Instead, it is a story about Naaman, but the real heroes who bring about the transformation of Naaman are the minor characters that surround him—the Israelite servant girl and his servants who accompany him to the prophet. The result of their actions is his cure and conversion. In the end there appear to be two points in preaching this story, which are related in a paradoxical way. First, God is indeed active independently beyond the boundaries of the people of God—for whatever reason Naaman found favor with God. And second, the only way that God's independent activity can come into clear focus is through the people of God—the servant girl and Elisha.

The Response: *Psalm 30*

A Hymn of Thanksgiving

Setting. Psalm 30 is a hymn of thanksgiving over having been healed. Verse 2 reads: "O LORD my God, I cried to you for help, and you have healed me."

Structure. Psalm 30 separates into three parts. It begins in vv. 1-3 with praise to God for rescuing the psalmist. Verses 4-5 shift the focus from God to fellow worshipers when the psalmist calls for those around him to join in giving thanks to God. In vv. 6-12 the psalmist recounts his life changes and how God rescued him. This section closes with a summary statement outlining the purpose of divine deliverance: It is so that the psalmist can continue to praise God.

Significance. The central motif of healing provides a direct connection to the healing of Naaman. If the psalm is read as commentary on the story of Naaman, then the psalm extends beyond the boundaries of the Old Testament lesson because Naaman's confessional response to Elisha about the power of God to heal him is not included in the lesson. This response by Naaman occurs in II Kings 5:15.

New Testament Texts

The conclusion of Paul's letter to the churches in Galatia and Luke's account of Jesus' sending seventy (-two) disciples to prepare his way are quite different materials, but there is a striking point of contact between the otherwise different texts. At Galatians 6:6 Paul seems to advise congregations to support their teachers, and at Luke 10:7 Jesus' directions to the pairs of disciples includes a note concerning the merit of the missionaries to receive support from those among whom they labor. In both texts, however, there are a variety of other themes, and focusing on any of these items registers the differences between the readings.

The Epistle: *Galatians 6:1-16*

The New-Creation Way of Being

Setting. The reading includes the major portion of the last chapter of Galatians, but the verses of the lesson are from two distinct sections of the letter. From 5:13 through 6:10 Paul offers a compendium of ethical instructions. Then, in 6:11-18 Paul concludes his letter. Thus, our lesson is initially ethical directives—quite situational in nature, but by analogy or extrapolation the remarks are relevant to us today. In turn, we read the majority of Paul's farewell. Even in saying "good-bye," however, Paul's mind soars to theological heights.

Structure. One finds four distinct parts to the reading. First, in vv. 1-5 Paul writes of Christian living as he admonishes each Galatian to Christ-like responsibility for both self and others. This line leads to a statement on generosity and the reasonableness of providing support for Christian workers (v. 6). In turn, in vv. 7-10 Paul offers further advice aimed at good inner-church relations. Here, we find the well-known maxim, "You reap what you sow." The verses are a call for the Galatians to give their lives to the will and the work of the Holy Spirit for the good of all believers. Finally, we encounter lines from Paul's "autograph" closing (vv. 11-16). Another call to the Galatians beckons them away from law-observance to recognition of grace in the cross of Christ. Thus, Paul's last concern is to remind the readers that it is not human effort but divine will experienced as grace that marks out God's people.

Significance. Paul admonishes the Galatians to deal gently with those who do wrong, for all go wrong at times. Yet, this is more than a charge to be nice. Notice that Paul refers to the Galatians having received the Spirit, and he refers to "the law of Christ." The Galatians fulfill Christ's standards as the Spirit empowers and moves them to deal with those who are in error. According to Paul, to commit our lives to Christ is to be done with the self-deception of arrogance and to exercise our God-given gifts for our Lord. Whatever pride Christians have should be in our obedience, not in our capacities, for our obedience is merely our yielding to the Spirit, not activity from our own initiative.

Next, in v. 6 Paul calls the Galatians to generosity. The statement is ambiguous, but Paul seems to say that Christians live generously, and they share with one another in all ways. Moreover, Paul says that those who teach are generous in that they share vital, edifying information. Thus, those who learn respond to their teachers' generosity by sharing what they have with them. Exactly what Paul means regarding the Galatians is impossible to determine, so forming analogies in interpretation is tricky. Most interpreters understand that Paul is informing the churches in Galatia that they are to support their teachers. Unless preachers want simply to make a pitch for a bigger salary, the reflection on this verse may lead to commenting upon the churches' benefit from supporting its schools and its students in training for ministry.

Verses 7-10 are clear, although consulting a theological dictionary about Paul's use of "flesh" and "Spirit" will bring further insights. Paul reminds the Galatians that they cannot fool God. When we focus on ourselves, even in God's name, we have the wrong focus and we stand condemned. Involvement with the Spirit is the proper way of life for believers, and the Spirit in our lives produces God's results. Paul recognizes that at times it is hard to do the right things, but he encourages the Galatians by reminding them that concern for God's will ensures the right results. (Here, Paul is especially thinking about good relations among the members of the congregation.)

Galatians was taken down by a scribe with specially trained ears, eyes, and hands; but Paul recorded his concluding comments in his own writing. He declares that observance of the religious law is an avoidance of the danger and the scandal of the cross; it is an easy way to feel religious while doing nothing—indeed, while dodging real Spirit-directed responsibility. Paul exposes the false glory of those advocating circumcision (and law-abiding righteousness) by pointing to the real glory of self-sacrificing love—God's love and the power of the Spirit in the lives of Christians. Paul declares that circumcision is truly a vain act in the context of God's new creation, for the new creation is a reality brought into being through God's work in Jesus Christ and in God's continuing labors by the Spirit. God's true people are those who obey God's will, not merely those who mark out themselves.

The Gospel: *Luke 10:1-11, 16-20*

The Way and Results of Christian Missions

Setting. Readers may consult the comments in setting for last week's Gospel lesson for general information on the broad context in which this week's lesson occurs. At present, we should recall that in an earlier part of his ministry Jesus had sent out the twelve for missions work (9:1-6). Now, on the "way" to his forthcoming Passion, Resurrection, and Ascension in Jerusalem, Jesus sends out a large number of his disciples to prepare his way. A textual problem makes it uncertain whether Jesus sent seventy or seventy-two disciples. The oldest and best manuscripts are evenly divided, so that the matter remains irresolvable. Nevertheless, in the context of Luke's Gospel we should not fail to notice that this sending is a dramatic acting out of Isaiah 40:3-5, a prominent part of the eschatological preaching of John the Baptist as remembered in Luke 3.

Structure. The lesson presents portions of the story of Jesus' sending of seventy or seventy-two disciples out in teams of two. Interpreters judiciously conclude that Luke has assembled originally disparate elements of Jesus tradition to construct a coherent speech to Christian missionaries at the point of their being sent out on mission. The entire story has the following structure: First, vv. 1-12 recall Jesus' sending of disciples. This account is Q material (Matthew and Luke's common source) and has partial parallels at Matthew 9:37-38; 10:16, 9-10*a*, 11-13, 10*b*, 7-8, 14-15. Second, vv. 13-15 find a parallel in Matthew 11:21-24. Luke seems to have brought these verses to their current context in his version of the gospel, so that they foretell the resistance to Jesus' emissaries and recognize the real difficulties that Christian missionaries meet. Third, v. 16 has a parallel at Matthew 10:40. Fourth, vv. 17-20 are without parallel in Matthew, but they are in part similar to material found in the longer ending of Mark (16:9-20, see especially 16:17-18). In general, Luke's efforts in fashioning these materials point to the importance of this speech.

Significance. Notice Luke's manner of referring to Jesus in v. 1; for Luke Jesus is clearly "the Lord," and as we observe his words and deeds in Luke's story of his ministry we should never forget that we are encountering the ways of our God. Here, Jesus deliberately and dramatically commissions seventy or seventy-two disciples to engage in missions in teams of two. We should probably relate Jesus' action to Moses' commissioning of seventy (or, seventy-two) elders in Numbers 11.

That the disciples are sent out in pairs shows us that even at its simplest level, Christian missions is never a solo voyage. Christian existence and Christian life are corporate in nature, for Christ calls us into life and action as God's people, not merely as God's persons. In turn, as Jesus sends out these teams he speaks deeply ironic words, telling them that the harvest is ready and great but the workers are few. We should not forget that Israel was a religious nation. Religious concerns and practices colored the fabric of everyday life, but Jesus says despite the religious cast of life and the number of religious leaders there were few workers available for God's work. The saying reminds us that religious activity that is merely directed toward God and not directed by God may be useless.

Further sobering words are spoken as Jesus recognizes the peril of the mission in which the disciples engage. They must trust God for everything as they labor to establish God's peace. The pronouncing of "peace" is not a type of Christian magic, rather it is a bold recognition of the power of God at work in the ministry of the disciples. God, not the disciples, is the source of the power of the work they do. Thus, the mission is to be forthright. The missionaries are not to aim at upward mobility through their service, for God works consistently and for the good of all humans, not merely to improve the lot of the disciples. Finally, Jesus' words of commission include a recognition of God's judgment of the rejection of the missionaries' message of Christ's coming. One sees this judgment symbolized in the wiping of dust from the missionaries' feet and their parting declaration, "The Kingdom of God has come near."

When the disciples return they tell of success despite the anticipated resistance. God's power and will prevail; yet, as we see, the struggle is real. Nevertheless, the success of the mission promises God's achievement of God's will. This success is not a call to triumphalism, rather the returning missionaries' are told to celebrate their faithfulness.

Proper 9: The Celebration

The Old Testament's image of cleansing and the epistle reading's reference to the new creation provide an appropriate scriptural setting for the administration of holy baptism today. These are united in the hymn, "Love Divine, All Loves Excelling," in the lines, "Finish, then, thy new creation; / pure and spotless let us be." If baptism is to be observed, then the Gospel reading may be changed to Luke 5:12-14, which does not appear otherwise in the lectionary. This story of Jesus healing the leper can stand in parallel to the healing of Naaman.

The statement in Galatians 6:8 about reaping corruption from the flesh if one sows to the flesh can be illustrated by today's Old Testament reading if it is extended to include the narrative about Elisha's servant, Gehazi, who sought to claim for himself the gifts that Elisha had refused as a reward for healing Naaman. The story itself may be told as an illustration even if it is not included in the actual reading.

The following lines, adapted from Isaac Watts and sung to Darwall's 148th, are a fitting response to the Gospel reading:

Now let our souls arise,
and tread the tempter down,
our Captain leads us forth
to conquest and a crown.
We feeble saints shall win the day,
though death and hell obstruct the way.

Should all the hosts of death,
and powers of hell unknown,
put their most dreadful forms
of rage and mischief on,
we shall be safe, for Christ displays
superior power, and guardian grace.

On this Sunday near the Fourth of July the preacher may wish to explore how the various issues of nationalism in the Naaman story end up taking second place to the work that God does. It is the minor characters in the story, the little captive and Naaman's servants, who do not let national or ethnic pride cloud their vision. Care should also be taken that the opening hymn is addressed to God, not to the nation.

Proper Ten Sunday Between July 10 and 16 Inclusive

Old Testament Texts

Amos 7:7-17 is the account of the vision of the plumb line by the prophet Amos and his confrontation at the Bethel cult site with Amaziah. Psalm 82 is a vision of God's appearance in the assembly of the gods.

The Lesson: *Amos 7:7-17*

The Plumb Line

Setting. The vision of the plumb line (7:7-17) and of the basket of fruit (8:1-12) will constitute the Old Testament lessons on Amos for the next two weeks. The reader will find the commentary on the setting of these two texts interrelated and hence interchangeable. The focus for this week will be on the prophet Amos, and next week on the form-critical category of a vision.

Amos 7:7-17 provides five pieces of information about the prophet, which are important for interpreting the book. First, the prophet's city of origin is considered to be Tekoa, a town south of Jerusalem by approximately fifteen miles. Thus Amos is a southerner or Judahite prophet. Second, the setting of the book is not the southern but the northern kingdom. Thus it would appear that this southern prophet has journeyed north to deliver a word of judgment. Amaziah makes this clear in 7:12-13 in his retort to Amos: "O seer, go, flee away to the land of Judah, earn your bread there, and prophesy there; but never again prophesy at Bethel, for it is the king's sanctuary, and it is a temple of the kingdom." Third, the message of Amos is not delivered just any place in the northern kingdom, but explicitly in a worship setting at the Bethel cult. Fourth, Amos is identified as a shepherd (Hebrew, *noqed*). This imagery has influenced a perception of the prophet as being someone that God suddenly whisked from the farm with an urgent prophetic ministry. This view has been reinforced with the exchange in 7:14-15, when Amos responds to Amaziah, the king's cultic priest at the northern city of Bethel, that he would not return to southern Judah as the priest suggests that he do, because he was "no prophet, nor a prophet's son; but . . . a herdsman, and a dresser of sycamore trees." The imagery here upon first reading appears to be of a spirit-filled lay person standing his ground against the crusty religious establishment. But the imagery may be more of a modern mythology than an ancient one. The exact meaning of the Hebrew word for shepherd is notoriously difficult to determine. It is not the common word for shepherd (Hebrew, *ro'eh*), and, in fact, the word occurs only one other time in the Old Testament, as a description of the King of Moab in II Kings 3:4. He is described as a "sheep breeder" (Hebrew, *noqed*), "who delivered one hundred thousand lambs and the wool of one hundred thousand rams" (AP) to the northern King Jehoram. So Amos and a king are the only two persons described with the term *noqed* in the Old Testament. The matter becomes even more complicated because of the occurrence of this word in ancient Canaanite/Ugaritic texts, where it is used in the same context as priest, which may suggest that a special class of "sheep herders" was part of the temple or cultic personnel. The fifth and final insight about Amos is the description of him as a visionary. In 1:1—which was originally a part of the lectionary reading, but has subsequently been dropped—Amos' prophetic activity is described somewhat paradoxically as the "words of Amos . . . which he saw." The Hebrew word used to describe seeing in this context is a technical word designating prophetic clairvoyance (Hebrew, *hazah*), and this word reappears in 7:12, when Amaziah also addresses Amos as a seer (Hebrew, *hozeh*). This designation is especially important for interpreting the two Old Testament lessons that have been chosen from the book of Amos, since both of these texts are classified as visions rather than prophetic oracles. The central goal for preaching is to determine just what it is that Amos sees.

The brief sketch of what can be gleaned about the prophet suggests two points of caution: (1) that preaching from the book of Amos ought not begin from the all-too-common idealization of him as an anti-institutional lay prophet, who has left the field to deliver his spirit-filled prophetic message to the king and his cult; and (2) that the content of his message is anti-worship in favor of strong ethical action. With regard to this final point, we must conclude that the only clear setting for the prophet's oracles is, in fact, worship (at the Bethel cult site).

Structure. The book of Amos can be divided into four parts. Amos 1:1–2:5 includes oracles of judgment against seven nations—Damascus, Gaza (Philistines), Tyre (Phoenicians), Edom, Ammon, Moab, and Judah. Notice how each oracle begins with the same phrase, "Thus says the LORD: For three transgressions of _____, and for four, I will not revoke the punishment." These oracles against other nations are presently structured ironically, because they lead unexpectedly into the second section of the book (2:6–6:14) when Amos turns what had been rather comfortable judgment oracles against other nations into a judgment oracle against Israel: "Thus says the LORD: For three transgressions of Israel, and for four, I will not revoke the punishment" (2:6). In contrast to the preceding oracles of judgment, which were limited to a paragraph, Israel's condemnation takes four chapters. Amos 7:1–9:10 switches from oracles of judgment to five prophetic visions: a plague of locusts (7:1-3), a fire out of control (7:4-6), a plumb line (7:7-9), a basket of summer fruit (8:1-3), and the presence of God by the altar (9:1). The final section in 9:11-15 switches somewhat surprisingly from intense judgment of the northern kingdom to an oracle of future restoration of the southern Davidic monarchy. This epilogue would appear to be a later addition to the book, which addresses the problem of the exile instead of the fall of the northern kingdom.

Significance. Amos is one of the strongest voices for social justice in the Old Testament. His central message to the northern kingdom was one of judgment: because they had abused righteousness and perverted justice (see, for example, 2:6-8), God was planning to destroy them (5:27). Amos 7:7-17 must be read with this central message as its background. Yet the text is difficult to preach because the genre is mixed. What starts off clearly as a vision in vv. 7-9 is now fashioned into a biography in which Amos and Amaziah clash at the Bethel cult in vv. 10-17. The problem is whether to focus on the vision and its meaning or the biography of the prophet and his conflict with Amaziah at the Bethel cult. The present interpretation will focus on the biography of the prophet and his conflict with Amaziah as an avenue for interpreting the vision.

The argument by Hans Walter Wolff (*Joel and Amos,* Waldemar Janzen, trans., in Hermeneia: A Critical and Historical Commentary on the Bible, Dean McBride, ed. [Philadelphia: Fortress, 1977]) that Amaziah is the point of focus in the exchange of 7:10-17, rather than Amos, will provide our departure for interpretation. The problem with Amaziah is that, unlike Amos, he lacks prophetic clairvoyance. His blindness is quickly illustrated by his response to the vision of Amos. Two exchanges are noted. The first is between Amaziah and the king in vv. 10-11 and the second between Amaziah and Amos in vv. 12-13. Both exchanges illustrate how Amaziah interprets the vision of Amos solely from a political point of view. He first reports to the king that Amos is speaking treason, and then he tells Amos to entertain visions where he is paid to do so, namely in Judah. In both of these exchanges the possibility of a divine word breaking in on the worshiping community at Bethel is rejected out of hand by Amaziah. Thus he is blind and doomed.

The response of Amos in vv. 14-17 is meant to illustrate the blindness of Amaziah. It separates between two statements, each of which includes a three-part series. First Amos states three things about himself in the first person: I am not a prophet, I am not the son of a prophet, I am a dresser of sycamore trees (v. 14). The end result of these three affirmations is that Amos has denied any authority in his conflict with Amaziah either in himself or in his position. In other words the prophet is eliminating himself from the conflict with Amaziah. The next three statements shift the focus from the prophet (with the "I" statements) to God: God took me from the flock, God said to me, "Go!, Hear the word of the LORD." If the first three "I" statements were meant to eliminate the person, Amos, from the conflict with Amaziah, then these final three statements are meant to provide the real point of focus for the conflict. Note how the first statement links Amos and God, but by the third, the prophetic personality is absorbed altogether in the divine oracle ("Now therefore hear the word of the LORD"). Amaziah, however, could not possibly hear this word, because he cannot see beyond the prophetic personality of Amos. The result is that the divine oracle never really comes into focus and Amos is evaluated solely within a political context. The blindness of Amaziah ensures his fate, which is graphically described in v. 17.

This conflict between Amaziah and Amos provides commentary on the vision of the plumb line. The plumb line is meant to test the sturdiness of the wall. It is not itself an instrument of judgment, but it does have the power to bring into clarity structural weakness. The conflict between Amos and Amaziah has functioned much like a plumb line, since it has brought into clarity the weakness of Amaziah (his blindness to see beyond Amos) and the strength of Amos (his ability to become absorbed in the divine oracle and hence to see visions). The preacher may wish to explore the power of blindness in Amaziah and how it prevented him from seeing beyond the power of the personality in front of him. From such a perspective Amos could only be an ally or an opponent. He could not possibly be a channel for a divine oracle or vision. As such his confrontation with Amos has been a test that has revealed his fundamental weakness, much like a plumb line would do in assessing a wall.

The Response: *Psalm 82*

A Call for Justice

Setting. Psalm 82 incorporates aspects of several different genres. It begins with a vision of God enthroned in the counsel of gods, but then speech becomes reminiscent of prophetic discourse, before the psalm ends with a plea.

Structure. The shifts in speech provide the contour for an outline of Psalm 82 into three parts: v. 1 vision, vv. 2-7 an indictment of the gods, and v. 8 a plea for divine justice.

Significance. Psalm 82 provides a countervoice to the blindness of Amaziah. The point of view of the psalm is visionary. The psalmist has entered into the divine counsel, and from the perspective of heaven, sees how the world and even all divine beings are held accountable to God to maintain justice and righteousness.

New Testament Texts

The opening verses of Colossians are elegant lines, filled with theological declarations and assumptions, all of which are solid themes for preaching. The material from Luke presents one of the best-known and most-appreciated stories ever told, the parable of the good Samaritan, a lesson in the meaning of God's compassion.

The Epistle: *Colossians 1:1-14*

Being Filled with God's Grace

Setting. In geographical terms Colossae was the least significant city to which one of the thirteen canonical letters attributed to Paul was written. In the mid-first century this former city had declined into a small town, which was destroyed by an earthquake in 63 C.E. and apparently never rebuilt. The letter itself indicates that the Colossians were enamored or were in danger of being enamored of a strange syncretistic religio-philosophy based on wisdom speculation. Colossians 2:8 refers to the "philosophy" and 2:23 makes clear the ascetic tendency of the thought and practice. In turn, 2:18 shows that somehow, someone thought and taught that through self-abasement the Colossians could experience "the worship of the angels"—most likely meaning "to join the angels in worship." Moreover, the practice of achieving ecstasy through self-denial had been mixed with the teachings of Christianity. The letter seeks to correct and to clarify the situation.

Structure. Colossians combines large sections of theological and ethical instruction. At times one wonders whether a statement is doctrinal or practical or both. The reading for this Sunday includes verses from the letter's salutation (1:1-2), thanksgiving (1:3-8), and body (1:9–3:17)—that is, the more doctrinal sections of the letter. The salutation includes the normal three elements of an ancient letter's opening: sender, recipients, and greeting. The thanksgiving is doxological language focusing on the faith and faithfulness of the Colossians. Verses 9-11 are a coherent unit of thought, despite the versification and paragraphing of the NRSV. In Greek the words translated "while joyfully" at the end of v. 11 are literally "with joy" and should be read with the first words of v. 12 as a new sentence—"With joy giving thanks."

Significance. The letter names Paul and Timothy as the co-authors of the writing, and interpreters such as Eduard Schweizer suggest that in this instance Timothy had more to do with the composition of the epistle than did Paul. The mention of Paul and Timothy and the way that they are named, "an apostle of Jesus Christ through the will of God" and "our brother," matches II Corinthians 1:1*a* exactly, so that such suggestions are but theories attempting to account for the non-Pauline elements in this thoroughly Pauline writing. The letter greets the Colossians as "saints and faithful brothers and sisters in Christ." Saints are "holy ones" who are made holy by God's own sanctifying work in Jesus Christ. Thus, designating the Colossians in this manner is a recognition of God's transformation of their lives, not a title referring to their goodness. Yet, the description of the Colossians as "faithful brothers and sisters" does recognize the character of their lives as they live related to God's grace. Thus, the greeting follows, "Grace to you and peace from God our Father," wherein "grace" designates God's work and "peace" refers to the outcome of God's activity.

The thanksgiving of the letter is striking. Thanks are given to God for the faithful lives of the Colossians. They live in such a manner that their living is characterized by faith, love, and hope. Trust in God invigorates a life of service that stretches forward toward God's promised future. The thanksgiving assumes that God's grace is at work bringing such lives of faith into being. Therefore, thanks are due to God, not merely a word of congratulation to the Colossians. The authors have the God-given capacity to look at the real lives of a congregation and to identity and articulate the presence and power of God at work among the believers. Thus, the thanksgiving models a theological reading of reality that may suggest doing a theological analysis of the life of congregations today. When we look at our churches, what evidence do we find of God at work among us as we live day to day? Is there faith? Is there love? Is there hope? If so, we need to recognize and thank God for the grace that produces these dimensions of our lives.

The body of the letter commences with the authors expressing their desire for the Colossians to be filled with the knowledge of God's will. Filled with God-given wisdom and understanding, believers naturally live in accordance with God's will. This is not to say that good information guarantees correct action, but rather wisdom and understanding are the results of the presence of God in our lives. In turn, God's presence and power transform our lives into an existence that is "worthy of the Lord." What God wants and expects of us, God gives to us in grace.

The Gospel: *Luke 10:25-37*

The Good Samaritan or Being Called Beyond Yourself

Setting. Following the return of the seventy (see last week's lesson), Jesus thanked God for the achievement of God's gracious will. Then, he pronounced a blessing on the disciples in recognition of their witnessing God's work. Luke introduces a new moment in the story with the first verse of our lesson. A lawyer—that is, an authority on the Jewish law—challenges Jesus. Luke's language shows the question of the lawyer to be hostile, not neutral. Even after Jesus handles the question concerning the inheritance of eternal life, the lawyer continues to press Jesus by asking about the identity of one's neighbor. Jesus tells the parable of the good Samaritan and, then, there is a brief dialogue.

Structure. The lesson shifts focus and genre repeatedly by moving from a brief narrative introduction to a question by the lawyer. Jesus answers the question with another question. The lawyer answers and Jesus affirms the reply and charges the lawyer to action. Then, the lawyer asks still another question to which Jesus responds by telling the story of the good Samaritan. The parable is episodic in character. After the story Jesus puts a further question to the lawyer, and when the answer comes Jesus again charges the lawyer to action. The structural complexity of this lesson is dynamic. While it may be impossible to recast the structure in preaching, the dynamic force of the verses, from question to demand for action to story, should inspire dynamic proclamation.

Significance. Hospitals bear the name of the Good Samaritan. Charity organizations describe their work using his name. People with only a minimal knowledge of biblical literature know his name and often this story itself. Endless sermons have been preached on this passage. What is there left to say?

Some observations may help to stimulate reflection for preaching: First, the story is not an allegory. Many sermons have looked for concrete characters or situations to explain the hidden meaning of the text, but interpreters and homileticians have abandoned allegorical readings of the parable.

Second, Luke frames the story situationally and reports a brief dialogue after the parable that gives particular force to the story. The initial exchange between Jesus and the lawyer is a controversy. After the parable, the dialogue ends in a clear commission.

Third, it is possible to handle the parable somewhat abstractly. For example, Martin Luther King, Jr., preached about three philosophies on the road to Jericho: "What's yours is mine"; "what's mine is mine"; and "what's mine is yours." Christ himself embodied the third philosophy and as Lord calls his disciples to this outlook on life.

Fourth, it is possible to observe the dynamics of the story of the good Samaritan and by analogy to rethink the meaning of the parable for people today. As the lawyer confronted Jesus about the religious perspective and the way of life to which he called his hearers, Jesus confronted the lawyer with a test of his identity by telling this parable. Jesus' story contrasts the priest and the Levite, identifiable Jewish leaders, with the resented, even hated figure of the Samaritan. The lawyer heard the story and was asked to judge the actions of the characters in the parable. The lawyer deemed the Samaritan to be the real neighbor in the story, for the Samaritan was the one who had compassion. Jesus calls for the Jewish lawyer to identify with the outsider in the story, not with the lawyer's actual peers—the priest and the Levite. The lawyer is asked to rethink his identity, to lay aside the standards that had given him identity and security, and to become like the outsider—a doer of God's will, an agent of divine compassion. The lawyer is called beyond himself. He is challenged to be merciful, to embody God's love, not merely to be an authority about God's will. Fifth, other interpreters suggest that for understanding this parable it is helpful to identify with different characters in the story. Think through the various actions, motives, and reactions that the parable attributes to the man who was robbed, the robbers, the priest and the Levite, the Samaritan, and even the innkeeper. How do these compare and contrast with one another? Where are there analogies in life today?

Proper 10: The Celebration

The three lessons may be connected today by the thread of compassion, of concern for the needy. Amos' plumb line becomes the standard set by the good Samaritan against which we measure our own exercise of love (Colossians 1:4, 10).

St. Augustine, in a sermon to bishops, compared their ministry to that of the innkeeper. It is easily adaptable to the ministry of all Christians.

> The robbers have left you half-dead on the road, but you have been found by the Good Samaritan who was passing by; you have had wine and oil poured upon you, you have received the Sacrament of the Only-Begotten; you have been set upon his own mount, you have believed in Christ incarnate; you have been brought to the inn, you are in the care of the Church. That is why I am speaking. And what I do, we all do: our position is that of innkeeper. To that innkeeper it was said: "I will pay you back whatever more you spend, when I come through here on my return." If only we were at least spending our own earnings! But everything that we are expending is the Lord's coin. We are your fellow-servants: we, too, live from what serves to nourish the rest. Let no one attribute to us the good that he or she receives. We are wicked servants if we do not give it; and if we do give it, then we still cannot boast about that, seeing that we are not giving of our own. (quoted in Michele Pellegrino, *The True Priest* [New York: Philosophical Library, 1968], p. 69)

Visuals today may include a plumb line and a first-aid kit.

The following adaptation of the salutation in Colossians may be used as a call to worship or as the introduction to the peace. The name of the local community should be inserted in place of Colossae:

> To the saints and faithful brothers and sisters in Christ in N.: grace to you and peace from God (our Father).

Colossians 1:13 may be adapted for today's Declaration of Pardon:

> God has rescued us [you] from the power of darkness and transferred us [you] into the kingdom of his beloved Son, in whom we [you] have redemption, the forgiveness of sins.

Verses 11-12*a* may form the Dismissal:

> May you be made strong with all the strength that comes from God's glorious power, and may you be prepared to endure everything with patience, while joyfully giving thanks to God.

Words of blessing or benediction should precede or follow the Dismissal.

The refrain and stanzas 2 and 3 of the hymn, "Jesu, Jesu, Fill Us with Your Love," may be used as a response to the Gospel reading.

Proper Eleven Sunday Between July 17 and 23 Inclusive

Old Testament Texts

Amos 8:1-12 is a vision of a basket of summer fruit. Psalm 52 is a psalm of lamentation that also includes aspects of prophetic judgment.

The Lesson: *Amos 8:1-12*

A Vision of the End

Setting. Amos 8:1-12 is the fourth of five visions in the book of Amos. The five visions include locusts in 7:1-3, fire in 7:4-6, the plumb line in 7:7-8, the basket of summer fruit in 8:1-2, and the destruction of the altar in 9:1. These five visions separate into three groups, the first two visions of judgment result in divine forgiveness, the second two foreshadow a coming judgment, and the final vision moves directly to a divine judgment. The first two visions follow a three-part pattern: (1) there is a description of what was seen, which is introduced with the words, "This is what the Lord GOD showed me" (locusts in 7:1 and fire in 7:4); (2) followed by an outcry from the prophet as a consequence of what he has seen ("O Lord GOD, forgive, I beg you!" in 7:2 and "O Lord GOD, cease, I beg you!" in 7:5); (3) finally there is a decision by God either to have compassion or to destroy. In the case of the visions of locusts and fire, compassion characterizes the divine response with the similar conclusion in 7:3 and 6, "The LORD relented concerning this; ' This also shall not be.' "

The three-part pattern continues with the visions of the plumb line and summer fruit, except that the outcry of the prophet in the second section is replaced by a divine question: (1) there is a description of what was seen, "This is what he (the Lord) showed me" (a plumb line in 7:7 and summer fruit in 8:1); (2) followed by a question to the prophet, "Amos, what do you see?" and the identification of the vision by the prophet; (3) in contrast to the preceding two visions there is not a decision by God to forgive. In fact, each vision portends judgment with the repetition of the phrase, "I will never again pass them by." But there is progression in this repetition toward the judgment in these two visions. In the case of the plumb line the vision would appear to be a test, with the outcome that it is not up to God to decide. Amos 7:8 simply states how God is setting a plumb line in the midst of Israel, even though 7:9 has now added a very specific outcome that does not really fit the vision. For this reason some scholars argue that Amos 7:9 is a later addition to the vision of the plumb line. The vision of the summer fruit takes the imagery a step further when God informs the prophet in 8:2, "The end has come upon my people Israel." The final vision in 9:1 moves directly from a (1) description of what was seen, "I saw the LORD standing beside the altar," to the (3) divine decision to destroy, "Strike the capitals."

This overview of the five visions illustrates the argument by Hans Walter Wolff (*Joel and Amos*) that there is design in the construction of Amos 7–9 from divine forgiveness (locusts and fire) toward divine judgment (altar), with the visions of the plumb line and the basket of fruit providing a transition toward judgment. This larger structure illustrates how the basket of fruit must be interpreted toward the end of this process. As such Amos 8:1-12 is best read as a series of prophetic indictments that are meant to confirm guilt.

Structure. Amos 8:1-12 separates into two parts. Amos 8:1-2(3) is the vision of summer fruit. Amos 8:4-12(14) consists of a series of prophetic judgment oracles that are meant to provide commentary on the vision in the present form of the text. This format of vision (8:1-2[3]) and additional commentary (8:4-12[14]) parallels the structure of the Old Testament lesson from last week, where a vision (7:7-8[9]) was also supplemented by biographical material (7:10-17) that was meant to provide an interpretation of the plumb line.

Significance. The central point of the vision in 8:1-2(3) is communicated through a word play in Hebrew. The word for "ripened fruit" in v. 1 is *qayis* and the word for "end" in v. 2 is *qus*. The relationship between the words for "ripened fruit" and "end" is homonymic, since the Hebrew roots actually come from different words. But the association of sound is enough to provide an interpretation of the vision. The ripened fruit (v. 1) is a vision of Israel's end (v. 2). Verse 3 makes this association explicit by introducing a funerary lamentation: "The songs of the temple shall become wailings in that day . . . ' the dead bodies shall be many, cast out in every place. Be silent!' " The strange call for silence is striking at the close of v. 3. It may indicate the fearfulness of the coming destruction as a number of commentators have argued. But, when the demand for silence is read in the larger context of the five visions, it may also be a command to the prophet to remain silent, and hence not to cry out in an attempt to avert the destruction as he did in the first two visions. The complete absence of a prophetic cry is what we find in the last vision of the altar in 9:1.

In place of the prophetic response of crying out to God at the horror of the vision, Amos presents a series of judgment oracles in vv. 4-14. Verses 4-7 present the full form of a judgment oracle, with the indictment in vv. 4-6 and the announcement of punishment in v. 7. It is important to note that the indictment of social abuse and exploitation in work practices is a repetition of the opening oracle of judgment in 2:6-7. Thus the book has come full circle in this penultimate vision. The remainder of the Old Testament lesson separates into three parts. The rhetorical question in v. 8 underscores how all the earth will tremble and mourn at the coming judgment of God on Israel—the land will tremble and everyone in it will mourn. Verses 9-11 take the reaction a step further by describing cosmological implications of the judgment—the sun will turn dark at noon. Finally vv. 11-12 explore the end result of judgment as an absence of God—people will wander but not find the words of God.

The book of Amos is a powerful message around two dark themes that can be explored in preaching. First, the repetition of judgment from 2:6-7 to 8:4-6 underscores how actions have real consequences. And, second, not all stories leave open the possibility of happy endings. The book of Amos illustrates, on the one hand, how there are, indeed, windows of opportunity in our interaction with God (the first two visions), but, on the other hand, how such opportunities are not permanent fixtures in the cosmos. The visions of Amos move toward darkness and not light.

The Response: *Psalm 52*

A Vision of the End

Setting. There is debate over the genre of this psalm. The opening verses have the mood of lamentation over the actions of evil persons, while the closing verses move to thanksgiving. Scholars shift their interpretation of the psalm between thanksgiving and lamentation depending on where the emphasis is placed. As a response to the Old Testament lesson an additional suggestion is worthy of reflection, namely that the psalm has incorporated aspects of prophetic judgment. As a prophetic judgment Psalm 52 provides another vision of the end.

Structure. The psalm divides roughly between vv. 1-7 and vv. 8-9. Lament and prophetic accusations dominate in the first section, while thanksgiving takes over in the final two verses.

Significance. Verses 1-7 take up the language of prophetic judgment. Verses 1-4 constitute a reproach or indictment. The evildoers are boastful, they plot destruction, lie, and love words that devour. This indictment culminates with judgment in v. 5. Note the disjunctive, But! God will break the evil ones down and uproot them. The opening section closes by switching to the perspective of the righteous person who has watched the downfall of the wicked. They will fear God and laugh at the evildoers. The psalm changes its mood at this point to conclude with thanksgiving by the righteous person.

The psalm provides an important response to Amos 8:1-12 for two reasons: it reinforces the judgment of Amos, while also taking the worshiping community beyond judgment. The first part of the psalm parallels the prophetic judgment that was central to the vision of the summer fruit. The conclusion, however, takes the worshiping community beyond the judgment of Amos with the language of praise from those who remained faithful to God.

New Testament Texts

The epistle reading is a highly poetic proclamation of the significance of the saving work of Jesus Christ and the implications or meaning of Christ's work for the lives of believers. The lesson from Luke is the familiar, but often troubling, story of Jesus' visit with Martha and Mary. The story calls disciples to distinguish the good from the necessarily better.

The Epistle: *Colossians 1:15-28*

Christ, Agent of Creation and Agent of Redemption

Setting. The verses of the epistle reading follow on the heels of last week's reading, so that readers may turn to the comments related to Colossians 1:1-14 for more extensive information. We find ourselves in the early portion of the body of the letter and the authors present their major theological argument related to the problems they perceive in the life of the congregation.

Structure. The verses fall into three distinct parts. First, vv. 15-20 record a lofty christological doxology that most interpreters take to be a hymn in praise of Christ. The meditation in this confessional piece concerns Christ as God's agent of creation and God's agent of redemption. Second, a pointed pronouncement of the meaning of the work of Christ for the readers of the letter comes in vv. 21-23. Then, third, vv. 24-28 register a series of observations. From the overt reference to "I, Paul" in v. 23 we find a recollection of the sufferings of the apostle in v. 24. Then, there is reflection on the apostle's service to God's divine commission (vv. 25-26). As the verses ponder God's commission they move to meditate on the presence of Christ in the lives of the believers.

Significance. The hymn in vv. 15-20 is an early Christian liturgical piece that declares the ultimate quality of Christ and his supremacy over all other powers. With few exceptions, interpreters understand that, here, Christ is confessed as being preexistent. Yet, even in this lofty praise Christ's preexistence is not passive being alongside God; rather, one finds that Christ is active as the Head of the Cosmos. The hymn focuses on Christ in two distinguishable but related movements: As Christ was active in creation, even so, now he is active as the Head of a new divinely created corporate entity—namely, the body of Christ which is the Church.

The composition of the Church according to these verses is quite striking, for it is made up of "all things, whether on earth or in heaven" that are reconciled in and through Christ himself. This cosmic view of reconciliation is a majestic statement of the magnitude of the saving work of Jesus Christ, and the preacher should be encouraged to declare boldly the wonder of Christ's accomplishment. The poetic, imaginative language is not our normal, more prosaic manner of expressing the meaning of God's work in Jesus Christ, so that frequently we shy away from proclaiming the marvel of redemption because of our own lack of an adequate, contemporary vocabulary and metaphor for declaring the wonder of God's work.

We may find stimulation for thinking about the meaning of this text for today if we notice that, on the one hand, the hymn proclaims Christ as the Head of Creation and the Head of the Church and, on the other hand, the hymn is informed by many unstated assumptions. Something that is not stated in this hymn happened after Christ acted to create all things in heaven and on earth. Somehow death entered the picture; there came to be a lack of peace; and a need for reconciliation came to be. In this situation the hymn celebrates Christ, the head of creation, acting as Christ, the agent of cosmic redemption. The hymn praises Christ, the head of the Church, who achieved victory over death, brought peace, and accomplished reconciliation. We should see that the hymn does not describe the problem; rather it declares and celebrates the solution.

In turn, vv. 21-23 take the verses of the hymn as a text and proclaim the reconciliation that Christ effected. As the author(s) shifts from "we" to "I, Paul" there is a hint of what is to follow in the ensuing verses. Now, the author bonds a firm admonition to the readers to be steadfast with the grand pronouncement of the accomplishment of redemption. The indicative declaration of Christ's work is coupled with an imperative to the readers to be steadfast, but we should see that as ever in biblical thinking the indicative precedes

the imperative. Yet, even in admonishing the readers to steadfast-
ness, the remaining verses of the lesson refer to the mystery of
God's word—the mystery that Christ is in the Christians so that they
have hope for faithfulness and future glory.

The Gospel: *Luke 10:38-42*

Choosing the Necessarily Better

Setting. With this story we find ourselves still on the way to
Jerusalem, to the time of Jesus' Passion, Resurrection, and Ascension. In this lesson Jesus comes with his disciples to a village where
a woman named Martha welcomes him into her home. Martha's sister Mary is present for the occasion, as apparently are Jesus' disciples.

Structure. The story unfolds in fine style. Initially, we locate Jesus
and his followers in a village on the way to Jerusalem, and then we
follow them into Martha's house. Martha clearly defines the space:
it is her house, so that all others including Mary seem to be guests.
Mary is defined in relation to her sister, although she acts independently by sitting at Jesus' feet to hear his teaching. Thus, Mary
assumes the posture and plays the role of a model disciple. By contrast, as the story continues, Martha is distracted from Jesus' teaching by the activities of hospitality. She protests, calling indirectly for
Jesus to rebuke Mary and to charge her to assist her sister in providing hospitality. Jesus refuses and instead gently, but clearly, rebukes
Martha as he praises Mary's choice of devotion to his teaching.

Significance. Our lesson tells a story that shows that persons concerned with embodying God's love will have nothing better to do
than to hear the words of Jesus Christ. The story directs disciples to
hear the teaching of Jesus above all else, for all else is secondary and
must follow in the wake of listening to Jesus' words.

What Martha does is good, but it is less than the best. All her service is lovely—although her call for a rebuke suggests that a tinge of
legalism motivates her elaborate performance of hospitality. Yet, all
Martha's efforts pale by comparison with the seemingly passive act
of listening to Jesus' teaching—the role Martha's sister, Mary,
elects.

Jesus' answer to Martha contrasts "many things" (good things) with "one thing" that is better because it is deemed "necessary." A clue for deeper understanding of Jesus' statement comes when we note at v. 41 that Luke again refers to Jesus as "the Lord." Thus, Mary attends to the one necessary action for true disciples: she hears the word of the Lord.

Jesus calls us to an active life of discipleship. Yet we are not merely set off for service that amounts to doing many good things. Above all, we are called to hear the word of our Lord, for only then are we equipped to understand his will and to undertake the multi-faceted service to which our Lord directs us. Indirectly, the story of Martha and Mary contrasts industrious service to the Lord with educated service for the Lord. From the entire context of Luke's Gospel we should see that merely listening is never an end in itself, but plenty of good work does not replace hearing and then doing the word of the Lord.

For preaching we should realize that most Christians will find it easier to identify with Martha than with Mary in this account. An engaging question for proclamation is "How would you have felt about things if you had been Martha?" Moreover, we live in a world that is recently and painfully aware that cultures socialize humans to take on certain roles as they grow up. Martha was doing what women were supposed to do, providing hospitality; and she was doing a major task by taking in Jesus and his disciples. We should recall that recently Luke has reported that at least seventy disciples were with Jesus on the road to Jerusalem. Martha takes on the preparations for a multitude while Mary takes a seat. How would we feel in Martha's place? Mary could have listened another time. Or could she? We should also recall that Jesus has set his face toward Jerusalem (9:51), so that he moves ever closer to his Passion. In Luke's story, the moment is a crucial one, and Jesus' call to discipleship places demands on the lives of those around him. Jesus' call to discipleship may even redefine traditional social roles, as was the case with Mary. Those who encounter Jesus are called to recognize the difference between what is good and what is necessarily better, and they are expected to act appropriately. Thus, while we can and should sympathize with Martha, we stand with her before Jesus and

we hear his words. Will we listen? Now, with whom will we identify—with Martha or Mary?

Proper 11: The Celebration

At first glance, today's three lessons appear to be so disparate in
theme as to call for the individual treatment of one to the exclusion of
the others. That is one option available to the preacher. There is another
possibility, however, if the preacher is interested in helping the congregation listen to the dialogue imposed by the passages. On the one hand,
we hear from the prophet Amos, the darling of Christian social activists
at least since the days of Walter Rauschenbusch, and on the other we
witness the passive receptivity of Mary, the darling of Christian contem-
platives since the days of the desert fathers. American Christianity has
often been pulled one way or the other in the last four decades of the
twentieth century by the differences between these points of view. The
Old Testament and the Gospel readings may be used to present the the-
sis / antithesis aspects of the debate. The epistle reading, however, provides for the synthesis in its declaration that in Christ all things hold
together (Colossians 1:17). This has always been the Church's answer
to the cynic's contention in whatever age that "things fall apart, / The
center cannot hold" (William Butler Yeats, "The Second Coming").
Tragically, both activist and contemplative become so convinced that
their particular approach to the gospel is the key to the world's salvation
that they forget that salvation is Christ's work, not ours, and our function is only to complement, to fill up (Colossians 1:24) what Christ has
done to save both the activist and the contemplative who are saved neither by their activism nor their contemplation.

Dorothy Sayers reminds us not to balance the Lukan text in such a
way as to negate the force of what Jesus has to say about the contemplative.

> I think I have never heard a sermon preached on the story of
> Martha and Mary that did not attempt, somehow, somewhere, to
> explain away its text. Mary's, of course, was the better part—the
> Lord said so, and we must not precisely contradict Him. But we
> will be careful not to despise Martha. No doubt, He approved of
> her too. We could not get on without her, and indeed (having paid
> lip-service to God's opinion) we must admit that we greatly pre-

fer her. For Martha was doing a really feminine job, whereas Mary was just behaving like any other disciple, male or female; and that is a hard pill to swallow. (Dorothy L. Sayers, *Are Women Human?* [Grand Rapids: Eerdmans, 1971], pp. 46-47)

The hymn, "Blessed Jesus, at Thy Word," is fitting for today's opening hymn or as a sung prayer for illumination prior to the reading of the lessons.

A response to the Gospel reading may be the following lines from John Wesley's translation of "Thou Hidden Love of God" (sung to St. Catherine or Vater Unser):

Each moment draw from earth away
my heart that lowly waits thy call;
speak to my inmost soul and say,
"I am thy love, thy God, thy all!"
To feel thy power, to hear thy voice,
to taste thy love, be all my choice.

Charles Wesley's "Jesus, All-Atoning Lamb" provides yet another response to the Gospel reading (suggested tune, St. George's Windsor):

Jesus, all-atoning Lamb,
Thine, and only thine I am;
Take my body, spirit, soul,
Only thou possess the whole!
Thou my one thing needful be;
Let me ever cleave to thee;
Let me choose the better part;
Let me give thee all my heart.

The middle of July will make it easy to provide a basket of ripening summer fruit as one of the visuals for today to reinforce the lesson from Amos. Notice that the imagery implied in the Hebrew (*qayis*) has to do with ripened summer fruit, fruit so ripe that it has turned the corner towards rotting. We are not celebrating harvest home here; we are being reminded that death is inherent in the natural order and that when we take pride in the full-bloom of life we are only seconds away from beginning the descent into the grave. As Colossians tells us, it is only the power of the redeeming Christ that can save us from that final destruction, and it is that redemption that we gather to celebrate as we recall the Paschal mystery from week to week.

Proper Twelve
Sunday Between July
24 and 30 Inclusive

Old Testament Texts

Hosea 1:2-10 is the account of how God commanded the prophet to marry Gomer, and it narrates the birth and naming of her three children. Psalm 85 is a prayer for divine favor.

The Lesson: *Hosea 1:2-10*

The Children of Hosea

Setting. The book of Hosea is rich in imagery and symbolic action. The prophet is commanded to marry a "wife of whoredom" and to have "children of whoredom," which he does in 1:2-10. This action sets up a variety of comparisons between the prophet, Gomer, children, and lovers on the one hand, and God, Israel, land, and competing gods on the other hand. The comparisons do not lead to clear and precise analogies, however. Thus the reader must be careful to avoid a too rigid interpretative framework for the shifting motifs. One comparison that does emerge quite clearly has more to do with the structure of the book than with the images and motifs within it. It is that the marriage of Hosea and Gomer in chapters 1–3 appears to be balanced by the oracles of judgment and salvation against the northern kingdom of Israel in chapters 4–14. The result of this is that chapters 1–3 provide the hermeneutical framework for interpreting the oracles in 4–14, hence the strong tendency toward analogy in the interpretation of the book of Hosea between Hosea and Gomer and God and Israel.

Structure. Hosea 1–3 separates into three parts. Chapter 1 recounts the marriage of Hosea and Gomer in prose. Chapter 2 shifts to poetry in order to describe the legal divorce proceedings between Hosea and Gomer. Finally, chapter 3 recounts the remarriage of the two. The lectionary text focuses on the initial marriage and the resulting children that are born to Gomer and Hosea. Interpretation will focus on the naming of the children, after the structure of the lectionary text is examined in more detail. Hosea 1:2-10 breaks into two very different parts. Verses 2-9 recount the marriage and naming of the children, all of which conveys an aura of judgment. Verse 10 is a statement of salvation. Smaller units emerge in vv. 2-9 by following the repetitive divine commands to the prophet: to marry (vv. 2-3) and then to name each of the three children (vv. 4-5, 6-7, 8-9).

Significance. Hosea 1:2-9 is about divine judgment on Israel. The message is not communicated through prophetic oracles, to which we are the most accustomed, but through symbolic actions. Hosea's use of this action is closely parallel to Isaiah, when the prophet is also commanded by God to marry a prophetess in 8:1-4, have a child, and name him Mahershalalhashbaz (meaning, "the spoil speeds, the prey hastens"). Three children are named by Hosea: a son Jezreel, a daughter Lo-ruhamah, and a second son Lo-ammi.

The aura of judgment is established in v. 2 with the repetitive use of the word *zanah,* which is translated in the NRSV as "whoredom." Hosea is to take a "wife of whoredom" and have "children of whoredom" because the "land commits great whoredom." The Hebrew word, *zanah,* can mean prostitute, but that is a derived meaning. Rather the word signifies unfaithfulness in a marriage relationship, which is not implicit to the notion of prostitution. The difficulty of interpreting Hosea is underscored in this verse when the reason for the command to marry is given as the fact that the "land" commits whoredom. "Land" could be a reference to the people (hence an analogy between Hosea-Gomer and God-Israel), but it need not, in which case *land* suggests some kind of relationship between God and earth. In the latter case the analogy in the book of Hosea is less focused on God's relationship with the people and more focused on God's relationship to the land itself through the central cult system. The ambiguity may very well be intentional in order to invite both readings, as the naming of the children would seem to suggest.

The first son is named Jezreel in vv. 4-5. The meaning of this name is the most ambiguous; it could be a reference to the land or to the people of Israel. On the one hand Jezreel is a statement about divine fertility in relationship to the land. It translates "May God sow!" or "God inseminates." The imagery of the name is one of divine procreation, and it may very well be functioning polemically against beliefs about Baal's fertility in Canaanite religion. Remember that in v. 2 it was the land that committed whoredom. The sexual imagery of the first name may very well be directed at worship practices in Israel where Baal, the god of fertility, was worshiped along side Yahweh. Such syncretism would not be a surprise, because official religion and popular religion are often meshed for pragmatic reasons. The Lord was certainly Israel's God, but the worship of Baal might be considered by prudent investors as an insurance policy. If the crops did not grow, after all, there were not vast refrigeration systems to carry the people through a period of famine. In its mildest form the worship of Baal might be no more offensive than the contemporary equivalent of the way in which many (if not all) believers confess the providence and care of God even while investing in insurance policies and a variety of tax deferred income credits for retirement. Such planning for security makes good pragmatic sense, but it also introduces variables in the life of faith, which create the potential for a conflict of interest concerning where our real security lies.

This background would suggest that one reading of the naming of the first child is to address the problem of security. Jezreel, then, is an affirmation that ultimate security (i.e., fertility) rests with God. In this case the attribution of fertility to Baal would turn the land itself (with its production of life-giving food) into whoredom. On the other hand, Jezreel could also be a reference to a specific location, which is then meant to symbolize what the people of Israel have become. As a location Jezreel was the second capital of the Omride dynasty. It was the place where Ahab killed Naboth, and where Jehu killed Ahab and Jezebel. It is a place of power politics, of blood, and of murder. All of these actions taken together symbolize how the people of Israel had come to embody action that indicated their unfaithfulness (whoredom) to God. The two readings of Jezreel are related in that each looks for security outside of God: One in nature religion and the other in power politics.

The next two children trace the outcome of Jezreel. The second daughter in vv. 6-7 is Lo-ruhamah. This name is translated "no mercy" or "not-pitied." That the child associated with this name is a daughter arises from the primary meaning of *rhm (ruhamah)* as womb. The word has feminine characteristics that become associated with God's most essential attribute, namely as being merciful and gracious (Hebrew, *rahum*—see the confessional formula in Exodus 34:6-7). The naming of the child as Lo-ruhamah, therefore, must be seen as a negation of God's most fundamental attribute, grace or forgiveness. The loss of divine forgiveness results in the naming of the third child, Lo-ammi, in vv. 8-9. This name signifies that Israel is a "non-people." This is not an image of holocaust, but one of non-ownership. Central to Israel's identity is its status as God's private possession (see Exodus 19:5). Because of Jezreel the prophet Hosea is proclaiming that the people have forfeited this privileged status.

The text provides a countervoice in v. 10, with imagery of restoration. The reason for the sudden and seemingly contradictory conclusion must be addressed in the commentary for next week on Hosea 11:1-11.

The Response: *Psalm 85*

A Prayer for Divine Favor

Setting. There is some debate over the genre of Psalm 85. Is it a lament as vv. 4-7 would suggest? But then how is one to read the opening three verses where some form of salvation has already been experienced by the worshiping community? Or are vv. 1-3 meant to be read in the future, as Herman Gunkel argued, in which case the psalm is a prophetic liturgy about a future salvation? We will follow those scholars who read the opening verses as a past event, which means that some initial form of salvation or divine favor is prompting the following petition.

Structure. Psalm 85 separates into three parts: the recalling of an initial experience of salvation in vv. 1-3, petition or complaint in vv. 4-7, and an oracle of salvation in vv. 9-12 that is introduced with the call for God to hear in v. 8.

Significance. Psalm 85 provides a response to the drama of Hosea 1. The motifs of remembering salvation in vv. 1-3 pick up the mood of restoration in Hosea 1:10. The difference between the two texts is that what was a future hope in Hosea 1:10 becomes a past remembrance for the present worshiping congregation, which is using Psalm 85 as a response to the Old Testament lesson. Once this connection is made, the core of the psalm becomes an identification with the message of judgment that is embedded in the naming of the children in Hosea 1:2-9. Verses 4-7 are a petition for God to forgive and restore life. Verses 8-12 move to a message of hope with an oracle of salvation. When read as a response to the Old Testament lesson, this conclusion brings the worshiping community back to the message of restoration in Hosea 1:10 from the same temporal perspective of looking for a future forgiveness.

New Testament Texts

The reading from Colossians explains the full significance of the Lordship of Jesus Christ: In him is all divinity, so that he is over all and incorporates all; therefore, "in him" Christians are freed from involvement with intermediaries and are set into direct relation to the divine. The lesson from Luke brings together a variety of materials, all of which are concerned with prayer. Jesus offers a model for prayer and, then, speaks words of assurance about God's hearing the prayers of those who pray.

The Epistle: *Colossians 2:6-15*

The Call to Life in Christ

Setting. At 2:4-5 the author explicitly states his desire to prevent the Colossians from being deluded. Then, the letter offers a two-part refutation of the "philosophy" among the Colossians. Our reading is the first part of the argument, and a second related part follows in 2:16-23. It is helpful, even crucial, to recall the problem being addressed by Colossians. The members of this congregation were becoming involved with a strange syncretistic religious philosophy based on wisdom speculation. Someone thought and taught that through self-abasement the Colossians could experience "the worship of the angels"—an ambiguous phrase that most likely means "to join the angels in worship." The situation seems to be that the practice of achieving ecstasy through self-denial had been mixed with the basic teachings of Christianity.

Structure. Three statements cohere in forming the argument in our reading. First, the letter calls the Colossians to faithful preservation of the origins of their faith (vv. 6-7). Second, vv. 8-10 exhort the readers to steer clear of any belief that compromises or denies the Lordship of Christ. Third, the argument reminds the Colossians of the origin of their faith in Christ and the vital meaning of the faith for the redemption of their lives; all is said with a clear christological cast (vv. 11-15).

Significance. Our reading has an intense focus on Christ Jesus the Lord, particularly as the readers of Colossians know him through the tradition that was taught them from the beginning. The letter calls for the Colossians to "live in [Christ Jesus]." That call is itself a mysterious sounding idea that may rightfully puzzle citizens of the twentieth century who are essentially unaccustomed to thinking and speaking in such terms. Fortunately the author explains the call by telling the readers they are to be "rooted" in Christ and "built up" in him. As they focus on Christ Jesus, as they devote their lives to him, the author says they will be established in faith. In other words, the letter to the Colossians calls the reader to a christocentric existence. Christ is more than a name, an idea, or a metaphor for the divine. Indeed, Christ is the reality of God's person, presence, and power; and Christians are called to give him central concern in the formation and living of their own lives. As one highly esteemed Christian leader once explained the course of his life, "Jesus Christ is more real to me than I am to myself." As the author of Colossians addresses his readers, his concerns are Christ as the focus, the foundation, and the force for life.

The lesson draws a sharp contrast between "human tradition, according to the elemental spirits of the universe" and tradition "according to Christ." The negative tone of the contrast should not obscure the author's assumption that Christian faith does have traditional content that is faithful to Christ. The language of the contrast is puzzling. What are "the elemental spirits of the universe"? The answer comes from examining the first-century mind as we know it through ancient literature. Indeed, the citizens of antiquity believed in a world larger than that visible to the human eye. The universe was thought to hold more than simply God and humankind. The elemental spirits of the universe were supernatural powers, forces, or beings who could influence the course of human life. Lower than God, the elemental spirits of the universe were recognized as being more powerful than humanity.

Notice that the letter to the Colossians does not deny the reality of such spiritual elements, but it calls the readers away from any concern with such forces. Colossians insists that since Christ is Lord of all, then, all created order is subject to him. If Christians have a relationship to Christ as Lord, then the elemental spirits of the universe have no claim and should have no influence on Christian life. Modern readers may not think of "the elemental spirits of the universe" in the same way that ancient persons did, but we do know larger social forces and structures that lay claims on our lives and seem to demand certain kinds of behavior that compromise our faithfulness to Christ. To us, Colossians says that faith in Christ sets us above such powers, for we are "in Christ" and he is Lord over all. Furthermore, Colossians declares that in Christ our lives are transformed. We experience change as the presence and the power of heaven itself—seen in the reference to resurrection in vv. 12-13—are identified as being currently real; they are not merely off in the future. In sum, the verses of the reading tell us that the recognition of the Lordship of Christ frees us from a sense of compulsion to reach out for God, for in Christ God has already reached out and grasped the lives of persons of faith.

The Gospel: *Luke 11:1-13*

The Lord and Prayer

Setting. The first verse of the lesson gives the context in which all the verses of our reading are to be viewed. The setting in life is perhaps more thematic than historical, for the materials that follow in vv. 2-13 are all related to prayer, although there are distinct pericopes in the lesson.

Structure. Three sections come together under the rubric of prayer. Verses 1-4 recall a request by a disciple and Jesus' giving of the model prayer. Verses 5-8 tell the parable of the importunate friend, a statement of assurance that God hears the prayers of those who pray. The final portion of our lesson, vv. 9-13, is a swirl of statements springing from and even building on the assurance given in vv. 5-8. While the materials are coordinated and thematically congruent, the parts of the whole lesson can easily stand alone. Only the boldest of preachers will dare take on the entire lesson, especially with any thought of dealing with the details of the various portions of the text. Nevertheless, the following comments touch on the entire lesson.

Significance. More than any other Gospel, Luke's account of Jesus' ministry recalls Jesus' regular practice of prayer. Clearly prayer was a vital part of Jesus' own life. Luke's own concern for the role of prayer in Christian life becomes clear as we read his account in Acts, which continues to report the prayer life of the earliest believers.

The waves of our lesson come onto the shore of a disciple's request that Jesus teach the disciples to pray. The urgency of the request is consistent with the urgent tone of the prayer Jesus gives to his disciples as a model. The prayer is poignant and brief. Matthew recalls a more elaborate or developed version of this same prayer (Matthew 7:7-11), which suggests but does not prove that Luke's form is older.

The address of the prayer is simple but profound, "Father." The directness of this address is daring and intimate. Unfortunately, valid contemporary sensibilities about the masculine cast of much biblical language cause us to miss the beauty of calling God "Father." We should imagine the best of all possible family relations and understand that we are directed by Jesus himself to approach God directly, simply, confidently, and affectionately. The point of this address is not an argument about God's maleness. Jesus and his disciples assumed the masculinity of God, but that assumption is not the point of this address in prayer. The challenge for preaching is to let the depths of this address inform our proclamation without allowing the problems of modern linguistics to obscure the truth of God's love. The matter will be poorly handled, however, by a flippant regendering of God as "Mother." Truth be told, there are plenty of bad mothers who can foul up the image of God as effectively as the bad fathers have.

Interpreters often point to the eschatological character of the opening petitions wherein the one at prayer beckons God with an urgency that reveals a yearning for the ultimate achievement of God's will and ways. The line (literally), "May your name be sanctified," is a stirring call for God to act, for God alone can establish holy reverence for God's name. Likewise, "May your kingdom come" (AP) is a cry for God to act. In turn, the petition for bread is an interpretive riddle. The words usually translated "daily bread" may well mean "bread for tomorrow." This sense would continue the eschatological or future tone of the foregoing line. Whatever the exact meaning, we should see how the prayer recognizes that our lives are sustained by God's own provision.

The final two petitions are related. First, the call for forgiveness recognizes God's ability to forgive human sin. The line is not, however, a statement about the conditions upon which God forgives; rather, it is a frank recognition that people who cannot or will not forgive have such a disposition that they cannot experience God's liberating forgiveness. Second, the petition concerning temptations recognizes that the present experience of grace (as forgiveness) is not a guarantee that life will be without difficulties in the future. God does not tempt humanity, but God alone—not we ourselves— has the power to direct us away from temptation into the life that God intends for us.

The second and third major portions of the lesson contain parabolic and metaphorical arguments "from lesser to greater." In the parable of the importunate friend Jesus works with the observation that between friends there are various reasons for granting requests—some more noble than others. Still, Jesus says, friends come through for friends even for selfish reasons. If that is the case, how much more can one count on God?

That point is made explicitly in the verses that complete the lesson. Jesus admonishes the disciples to ask, to seek, and to knock. There is no guarantee here that one will get a pink Cadillac because he or she prays for it; rather, Jesus offers a firm assurance that earnest prayers are heard. The assurance is underscored through comparing and contrasting evil earthly fathers with Jesus' heavenly Father. In the statement about God we see both the basis of the assurance and the reality for which Jesus expects the disciples to pray—namely, the Holy Spirit.

Proper 12: The Celebration

The commentary on both the Old Testament and epistle lessons indicates that a common concern, though separated by centuries, was that of syncretism, the effort to combine different faith or belief systems. In the first case it was the worship of Yahweh with that of Baal, and in the second it was fidelity to the Lordship of Jesus Christ with "religious" practices that were thought to induce spiritual experience. And although we are separated by yet more centuries from Hosea and Paul, the danger of syncretism remains ever-present in the Church's life. Syncretism may be defined for the Church as the courting of whatever culture in which it finds itself in order to hedge its bets and have the best of both worlds. Along these lines, preachers may be stimulated for today's sermon and for thinking about preaching generally by Stanley Hauerwas's provocative book *Unleashing the Scripture: Freeing the Bible from Captivity to America* (Nashville: Abingdon Press, 1993).

Paul suggests that our baptism into Christ releases us from captivity to human traditions—that is, the necessity of doing "what is expected of us" in order to maintain the norms of respectability or middle-class morality. The example of Hosea must have been seen as scandalous by his neighbors who doubtless knew very well what kind of example to the community a preacher ought to set. And Jesus himself hardly demonstrated a law and order mentality.

> The people who hanged Christ never, to do them justice, accused him of being a bore—on the contrary, they thought him too dynamic to be safe. It has been left for later generations to muffle up that shattering personality and surround him with an atmosphere of tedium. We have very efficiently pared the claws of the Lion of Judah, certified him "meek and mild," and recommended him as a fitting household pet for pale curates and pious old ladies. To those who knew him, however, he in no way suggests a milk-and-water

person; they objected to him as a dangerous firebrand. True, he was tender to the unfortunate, patient with honest inquirers, and humble before heaven; but he insulted respectable clergymen by calling them hypocrites. He referred to King Herod as "that fox"; he went to parties in disreputable company and was looked upon as a "gluttonous man and a winebibber, a friend of publicans and sinners"; he assaulted indignant tradesmen and threw them and their belongings out of the temple; he drove a coach-and-horses through a number of sacrosanct and hoary regulations; he cured diseases by any means that came handy, with a shocking casualness in the matter of other people's pigs and property; he showed no proper deference for wealth or social position; when confronted with neat dialectical traps, he displayed a paradoxical humour that affronted serious-minded people, and he retorted by asking disagreeably searching questions that could not be answered by rule of thumb. He was emphatically not a dull man in his human lifetime, and if he was God, there can be nothing dull about God either. (Dorothy L. Sayers, quoted in David Coomes, *Dorothy L. Sayers: A Careless Rage for Life* [Batavia, Ill.: Lion, 1992], pp. 129-30)

The point is well-made in today's Gospel reading when Jesus teaches about prayer. He does not expound some esoteric doctrine or give a complicated series of rules that must be followed if God is going to hear and respond. Rather, he says simply that talking to God is like family conversation where you express yourself unselfconsciously with the confidence that you will be heard and understood. And it is the life of prayer, of communion with God, that enables us to live out the consequences of our baptismal freedom without regard for the opinions of the elemental spirits of the culture. Prayer, then, is not a means of getting something; it is a way of being in relationship to God, and Christians ignore it to their own loss, since Jesus describes his Father in terms that come close to being an easy touch.

Why, therefore, should we do ourselves this wrong,
Or others, that we are not always strong,
That we are ever overborne with care,
That we should ever weak or heartless be,
Anxious or troubled, when with us is prayer,
And joy and strength and courage are with Thee?
(Richard Chenevix Trench, "Prayer")

Psalm 85 provides the title line for the gospel hymn, "Revive Us Again." Its chorus could be used today as the sung response or antiphon for the psalm. Or the whole hymn could be used to open or conclude the service.

The baptismal references in Colossians make today an appropriate one on which to schedule mid-summer baptisms.

Proper Thirteen Sunday Between July 31 and August 6 Inclusive

Old Testament Texts

Hosea 11:1-11 is rich in images of God as parent and God and destroyer, but it apparently functions as a divine soliloquy about forgiveness. Psalm 107 is a hymn of praise.

The Lesson: *Hosea 11:1-11*

Forgiveness

Structure. Hosea 11:1-11 is a notoriously difficult text to interpret because the Hebrew presents so many problems. Just a few examples will illustrate the point. In v. 2 the NRSV has translated, "The more I called them, the more they went from me." This translation makes perfect sense since it is a speech of God that reflects on Israel's past actions. The Hebrew, however, reads, "The more they called them, the more they went from them." Who is "them"? The same problems emerge in v. 3. The NRSV has continued the verse as a self-referential speech by God, "I took them up in my arms," even though the Hebrew translates, "I took them up in his arms." If you have an NRSV with notes, check the bottom of the page and you will find that significant problems in determining the meaning of the Hebrew continue in v. 4 ("who lift infants to their cheeks"), v. 5 ("I bent down to them and fed them"), v. 7 ("but he does not raise them up at all"), and v. 9 ("and I will not come in wrath"). Such problems are worthy of reflection, for they underscore how very ancient the Old Testament text is and how many hands it has passed through (including the NRSV translators) to reach a contemporary worshiping community. A brief overview of some recent commentaries will illustrate how this text has been interpreted as a statement of judgment (Francis I. Andersen and David Noel Freedman, *Hosea*, The Anchor Bible [New York: Doubleday, 1980]) or conversely a statement of salvation (Douglas Stuart, *Hosea-Jonah*, Word Biblical Commentary [Waco: Word Books, 1987]). The difficult choice depends on how you read the book as a whole. If you link Hosea 11 to Hosea 13, you emphasize judgment. If you link chapter 11 to Hosea 14:2-9, you emphasize salvation. The following interpretation will tentatively treat the text as a statement of salvation, and as such, Hosea 1:1-11 provides commentary and explanation for the sudden shift from judgment to salvation that was noted last week when Hosea 1:2-9 was compared to 1:10.

Structure. Hosea 11:1-11 separates into three parts. The text opens in vv. 1-2 and closes in vv. 10-11 with statements about Israel. Between these two sections vv. 3-9 present an extended soliloquy by God. The text can be outlined in the following manner.

I. Israel's Present Response of Disobedience to God (vv. 1-2)
II. Three Actions by God (vv. 3-9)
    A. God as past healer (vv. 3-4)
    B. God as present destroyer (vv. 5-7)
    C. God as forgiver (vv. 8-9)
III. Israel's Future Response of Obedience to God (vv. 10-11)

Significance. The goal for interpretation and for preaching is to determine how Israel's disobedience in vv. 1-2 is transformed into obedience by vv. 10-11. Clearly the answer lies in the activity of God that is sketched out in three parts in vv. 3-9.

Verses 1-2 provide the context for interpreting vv. 3-9. Thus the situation prompting the divine reflection is disobedience. This situation provides an easy transition from Hosea 1:2-10, where Israel's disobedience was described through the birth of the three children. The three sections of Hosea 1:3-9 (vv. 3-4, 5-7, 8-9) trace the action of God as a response to Israel's disobedience.

The imagery of God as a past healer in vv. 3-4 underscores

Israel's guilt. The verses play off the imagery of the Exodus that was noted in v. 1. The movement within the text is of Israel being led out of Egypt. The imagery is that of an infant or toddler, who is not self-sufficient. Thus, it is God who taught Israel to walk, who picked her up, and who healed her when necessary (v. 3). Verse 4 is unclear. If the imagery is one of an infant being lifted to a cheek, then God is being viewed as a parent. If, however, the verse is a description of freedom from a yoke, then Exodus imagery of liberation is being explored with God being pictured as Israel's liberator. In either case the imagery of a parent with an infant returns in the closing line of v. 4, where God is pictured as feeding or nourishing Israel most likely on the trip out of Egypt.

God becomes a destroyer in vv. 5-7. These verses are closely related to vv. 3-4 in a number of ways. Movement remains an important structuring device in the section, but it is reversed from the earlier section. Now Israel is described as returning to Egypt, instead of being saved from it (v. 5). And with this reversal in movement the imagery of God also changes. Instead of a nurturing parent, God is a raging sword (v. 6), whose food is no longer nourishment, but a devouring fire (v. 6). The reason for this series of reversals is that Israel refuses to return to God (v. 7). Thus the stage is set for justified divine judgment.

Verses 8-9 provide a surprising reversal. The cycle of action consisting of disobedience and punishment is broken when God reflects on the divine character: "I am God and no mortal." This statement suggests that God is not bound to cycles of action even when punishment is justified. Instead, the essential character of God as mercy or grace can break through and restructure all action. Two things are noteworthy for preaching this text. First, the breaking of the cycle by God is a reemergence of *rhm* (mercy) that was negated momentarily with the second child (Lo-ruhamah). Second, this surprising reversal of unexpected grace is paralleled in the trial scene of Hosea and Gomer in chapter 2, where the prophet also stops the divorce proceedings at the very moment when he has won his case. Hosea 11:1-11 suggests that we move from judgment to grace solely on the basis of God's character.

The Response: *Psalm 107:1-9, 43*

Giving Thanks for Forgiveness

Setting. Psalm 107 separates into at least two parts. Verses 1-32 are a song of thanksgiving and vv. 33-43 are a mixture of hymnic praise and wisdom sayings. The first section appears to have had a liturgical setting of praise in which a priest would have called a congregation to praise (v. 1) by providing four different situations in which the salvation of God could have been experienced by the worshipers (vv. 4-32). The four situations included those who traveled the desert and experienced the deliverance of God through food and direction (vv. 4-9), those hopelessly lost in prison who experienced the presence of God (vv. 10-16), those who were sick and recovered (vv. 17-22), and, finally, those who traveled the dangerous seas and experienced God's salvation by surviving a storm (vv. 23-32). The second part of the psalm (vv. 33-43) is meant to provide still more occasions of salvation that prompt praise to God.

Structure. The lectionary text separates into four parts: an introductory call to praise in v. 1, perhaps an extension of the call to praise in vv. 2-3, a response of praise by those who wandered in the wilderness at great danger in vv. 4-9, and a wisdom saying that functions as a conclusion in v. 43.

Significance. The central imagery in using Psalm 107 as a response to Hosea 1:1-11 is the giving of thanks for salvation from the wilderness in vv. 4-9. This section includes many of the motifs from the Old Testament lesson and recasts them as praise by the worshiping community. The motifs include traveling in the wilderness, being fed and nourished by God, and the merciful character of God.

New Testament Texts

The verses from Colossians call for the readers of the epistle to take seriously the dynamic workings of God in their lives and admonish them to focus their own living on doing God's will as God works in their lives. The exhortation of the epistle sounds across the centuries speaking to the life of Christians today. The parable from Luke's Gospel is a startling story about a man who lost his very soul because of his total devotion to his material possessions. In an affluent age of consumerism the parable reveals a frightening truth.

The Epistle: *Colossians 3:1-11*

Seeking the Things That Are Above

Setting. After the verses of the epistle reading for last Sunday, in Colossians 2:16-23 the author continues to refute the "philosophy" with which the Colossians have become involved. Then, the next segment of the epistle, 3:1-17, presents hortatory material. The exhortation is, however, still doctrinal in character and abstract in nature; so that in comparison to the practical materials that follow in 3:18–4:6 our reading is still a part of the body of the letter, not the letter's parenesis.

Structure. Our reading presents two of the final three units of the body of the letter. In vv. 1-4 the author instructs the Colossians to seek heavenly things because they are blessed with participation in the saving power of Christ's resurrection. The author explains in vv. 5-11 the kinds of "earthly" characteristics, attitudes, and activities that the Colossians are to shun, insisting that God's saving renewal of their lives in Christ eliminates former distinctions and patterns of relating to one another.

Significance. The new life of believers in Christ comes as the result of God's power, which raised Christ, grasping our lives. That is the good news! Yet, the transformation of our lives is not merely a passive experience, as is clear from the admonitions in our lesson for the readers to seek the things that are above—that is, heavenly things, attitudes, and actions typical of the presence of Christ as he is seated at the right hand of God. In turn, the reference to the right hand of God in relation to the admonition to seek heavenly things underscores the crucial operation of God's power in our very seeking.

Having called for the readers to strive toward God's ways and having recognized the active role of God's power in the transformation of our lives, the author explains in relatively practical terms how the divine re-formation of our lives occurs. We are called to set our minds on heavenly things, not the earthly. There are positive and negative dimensions to our experience of salvation—we focus on "this"; we do not focus on "that." In connection with the epistle's admonition to take on a proper focus we find a striking unpacking of the idea of being "raised with Christ." In the imagery of this letter, sharing in Christ's death is clearly experiencing a death to sin, and, in turn, to be raised with Christ is to have our new lives hidden with Christ in God. Indeed, Christ is the new life of believers. As God's work in Christ generates new life, believers live "in" the world, but by sharing in Christ's death and resurrection believers live a new life that is not "of" the world. Yet, such understanding of Christian life is not triumphalism—"we have the glory of the resurrection!" Rather, being raised with Christ means we have the assurance that God's work grants a new quality of life from "above," from beyond the mundane realities of mere human existence.

Put differently, the past does not determine the present, for God has been and is at work altering the quality of human existence. Moreover, the future is not equal to the present in a reduction of divine reality to realized eschatology. Our reading makes that point clear in v. 4. There is present transformation, and there is future glory. The two are related, but they are not to be equated.

The catalogue of "earthly" things with which Christians are to have nothing to do is illustrative, not exhaustive. The lists illustrate (1) that not all behaviors and attitudes are acceptable in terms of God's own standards and (2) that God's judgment of the unacceptable registers divine displeasure as God works to eliminate that which is contrary to God's will. Moreover, Christians are called to an active participation in God's elimination of the "earthly"—that is, all that is opposed to God's will. The epistle does not direct Christians to go out "sin-bashing"; rather, Christians are to rid their own lives of disobedience to God's will.

The Christian self is brought into a new relationship with God as our creator renews us by intimate involvement in our lives. Thus, old earthly standards are gone as Christ is established as the unifying center of our new corporate existence.

The Gospel: *Luke 12:13-21*

The Tyranny of Things

Setting. In Luke 12 we find Jesus teaching the multitudes that gathered around him as he made his way toward Jerusalem. In the summary statements about his words to the crowd that precede our lesson, we find Jesus warning against hypocrisy, promising God's ultimate and revealing judgment, calling for rightfu¹ fear of God in recognition of God's ultimate authority, and promising God's grace and care. Then, Jesus teaches about the power, presence, and work of the Holy Spirit. Above all, he promises those who are faithful disciples that the Holy Spirit will sustain them in times of difficulty. The variety of teachings forms a cluster, calling for the crowd to devote their lives to God in full confidence of the goodness of God's purposes.

As Jesus teaches the people in this way, Luke reports that a man from the crowd urged Jesus to direct his brother to distribute the family inheritance in an equitable fashion. Jesus refused, and, instead warned against the consuming destruction of life by avarice.

Structure. The heart of our lesson is the parable, vv. 16-21, a story that should disturb anyone who listens carefully. But this parable is told to the crowd only after Jesus' exchange with the man (vv. 13-14) and Jesus' subsequent warning against greed (v. 15). The parable is a caution that is coupled with an observation about the real substance of human life (v. 21).

The structure of our lesson mounts a critique of a life of sheer materialism. Jesus refuses to become involved with a controversy over "things." He shows no interest, and he denounces greed as a way of life lost to consumption or possession. In the end he calls for the formation of life in full concern with God.

Significance. Jesus seems less than fully sensitive when he spurned the man who asked for his assistance in achieving a "fair" sharing of the family goods with his brother. Commentaries help make sense of the request by describing the way possessions were inherited in Palestine: The oldest son received a double-share of the goods. The idea was to perpetuate the family name and wealth, not

111

to divide evenly. Jesus took no interest in the matter, refusing to question traditional inheritance laws. As he handled the issue, we see that he read an appeal for fairness as little more than a request from sheer self-interest. Nothing in the story suggests the man was greedy, but Jesus' statements show that he found the man's request inappropriate. Hearing the teaching of Jesus, the man thought about the poor deal he got as a younger son. Listening to Jesus talk about God's grace, the man assumed Jesus would want to help him get a bigger piece of the family pie. According to Jesus, the man was thinking about the wrong kinds of things, and he was in danger of letting greed get the best of him. When we learn about the inequitable inheritance laws, can we help sympathizing with the man? When we see the reasonableness of the man's request, are we scratching the surface of our own greed? Is there greed in our lives that threatens to cost us our lives? The story of the man's request and Jesus' response to him combine to call our attitudes, aspirations, and lives into question before God.

The parable itself is a strange, challenging story. Jesus focuses on the person of the rich man, indeed we know little else about this man except that he was rich. In antiquity wealth was nearly always associated with possession of property, particularly land; and so, when the parable tells us of the rich man's land providing abundant crops we are to understand that the already rich man has become even richer than he was. The rich get richer. But the parable tells nothing about the poor getting poorer. Interpretations of this story that fault the rich man for a lack of generosity are at best reading between the lines. Interpretations of this story that denounce the rich man for his insensitivity to the poor are simply reading into the text, for the parable never mentions or hints about the plight of the poor. This story is not the parable of the rich man and Lazarus, so let the rich fool be the rich fool.

God's calling the rich man a fool is one of the keys to understanding Jesus' story. The man's land produces abundantly, and observing the bounty the rich man destroys what he has to build himself bigger and better things. As the rich man talks to himself, we learn the purpose of his endeavor. He seeks to find his security and comfort in the abundant possessions he lays up for himself. "Fool," says

God; or as Jesus put it, the man chose to "store up treasures" rather than to live so as to be "rich toward God." What exactly it means to be "rich toward God" is a secondary question in relation to this parable, although in pondering this phrase one may think about a lack of generosity and even insensitivity toward the poor. From the other portions of Luke's account of Jesus' ministry we know that generosity and concern for the poor are vital concerns.

Nevertheless, the thrust of this parable is a critique of persons who live their lives with the wrong set of values or the wrong set of ultimate concerns. Inherent in this parable is a telling truth that is completely lost in translations. The NRSV (and all other translations similarly) render v. 20, "But God said to him, 'You fool! This very night your life is being demanded of you. And the things you have prepared, whose will they be?' " God's words, however, more literally say, "Fool! In this night they demand your soul from you. But the things you prepared, whose will they be?" Consider the statement. Who or what are the "they" that demand the foolish rich man's soul? In context, only "the things" can be the "they." The possessions own the man, the man does not own the possessions. Greed leads to an accumulation of material goods, and things ultimately control our lives so that we are not free to live toward God.

Proper 13: The Celebration

Themes from all three lessons are reflected in Charles Wesley's beautiful and moving hymn, "Jesus, United by Thy Grace," which should be sung to a meditative common meter tune such as St. Agnes.

1. Jesus, united by thy grace
and each to each endeared,
with confidence we seek thy face,
and know our prayer is heard.

2. Still let us own our common Lord,
and bear thine easy yoke,
a band of love, a threefold cord,
which never can be broke.

3. O make us of one spirit drink;
   baptize into thy name;
   and let us always kindly think
   and sweetly speak the same.

4. Touched by the lodestone of thy love,
   let all our hearts agree,
   and ever t'ward each other move,
   and ever move t'ward thee.

5. To thee, inseparably joined,
   let all our spirits cleave;
   O may we all the loving mind
   that was in thee receive.

6. This is the bond of perfectness,
   thy spotless charity;
   O let us (still we pray) possess
   the mind that was in thee.

If United Methodists use the hymn as it appears in their hymnal, they should note that it lacks the second stanza above with its reference to Hosea 11:4.

The mention of that omitted stanza raises the question of the use of hymns in sermons as illustrative material and as a means of introducing congregations to a wider canon of worship resources. Many of those who teach and influence worship practices in Protestant circles were raised in churches where it was customary to hear the minister announce, "We will sing verses one, two, and four." As one ecclesiastical satirist has put it:

If salvation's story
And heaven's great glory
Were contained only in each third verse,
Scarce an ear would have heard
That most life-giving word,
And we'd all still be under the curse.

Each song is thus trimmed
To three-fourths of a hymn,
As if there were time for no more,
And the meaning is trounced

Ev'ry time 'tis announced,
"We will now sing verse one, two, and four."

(Dr. Kirk Mariner, Mt. Olivet U.M. Church, Arlington, Virginia; used by permission)

The reaction to this kind of editing was to emphasize the integrity of the whole text and to insist that hymns should be used in their entirety. While that may generally be true for hymns in a liturgical context, it was never meant to restrict the use of selected stanzas to make a particular liturgical statement (as we have sought to illustrate throughout this series) or to illustrate some aspect of the sermon. The unfortunate result has been that congregations think of hymns as something that happens three times at most in a worship service (traveling music at the beginning and the end and a seventh inning stretch before the sermon). The use of a stanza may include the singing of it by a soloist, the choir, or the congregation rather than simply its quotation. Such a use will enlarge the congregation's knowledge of tunes and texts as well as give the sermon greater variety and interest.

"Sing Praise to God Who Reigns Above" is an appropriate opening hymn today with its reference to Hosea as well. Also, the gospel hymn, "I've Found a Friend, O Such a Friend," draws on Hosea for its imagery.

This or next Sunday will fall close to the anniversary of the bombings of Hiroshima and Nagasaki. Attention should be paid to the date by the use of appropriate prayers and readings.

Proper Fourteen
Sunday Between August 7 and 13 Inclusive

Old Testament Texts

Isaiah 1:1, 10-20 is a judgment oracle or perhaps better a disputation about worship. Psalm 50:1-8, 22-23 is a description of theophany that evolves into divine judgment.

The Lesson: *Isaiah 1:1, 10-20*

A Judgment on Worship

Setting. Isaiah 1 is made up of a variety of smaller (and most likely independent) units. Otto Kaiser, for example, in his commentary *Isaiah One to Twelve,* (2nd ed., in The Old Testament Library [Philadelphia: Westminster, 1983]) suggests that the chapter may be made up of no less than six separate sayings in addition to the superscription in v. 1 (vv. 2-3, 4-9, 10-17, 18-20, 21-28, 29-31). These speeches represent motifs that recur throughout the entire book of Isaiah (for example, Israel's lack of knowledge in vv. 2-3, red or blood as a symbol of guilt in vv. 15 and 18, and estrangement or alien as a description of Israel in vv. 4 and 6). The recurrence of these motifs as well as garden imagery associated with Zion (vv. 27-31) suggests that the chapter is meant to function as an introduction, analogous to an abstract or summary of key points in a report. Central to the chapter is a criticism of worship and its complete inability to influence moral behavior outside of the cult. This state of affairs is reflected in the tone of the chapter, which brings to mind a courtroom setting. Note how the opening oracle in vv. 2-3 describes God as presenting a case against Israel, with the heavens and the earth being the witnesses. This opening oracle is linked with a second in

vv. 4-8(9) in which Israel's activity is condemned through a woe oracle (vv. 4-6) and the results of this activity on the land are described through images of desolation (v. 7). With vv. 2-9 as background, the lectionary reading of vv. 10-20 focuses more specifically on the contradiction between the people's worship and ethical life.

Structure. The smaller units of prophetic discourse noted above have been shaped into a larger literary design in the present form of the text. Note, for example, the repetition of a call "to hear" divine speech in vv. 2 and 10. This repetition provides an initial clue for structuring the chapter. It begins with a superscription in v. 1, which is followed by an opening address directed to the heavens and the earth in vv. 2-9. The lectionary reading constitutes the second address directed to the rulers and people of Sodom and Gemorrah in vv. 10-17. Verse 18 most likely begins a new unit that continues through the end of the chapter (vv. 18-31). Verses 18-20 constitute the introduction to vv. 18-31. Note how the motif of hearing is repeated in v. 19 and how there is a repetition of the motif of divine speech in v. 20, as was the case in the other introductory verses (vv. 2 and 10). This introduction leads into an analysis of the present state of the city as being one of faithlessness (vv. 21-23) leading to a verdict of judgment (vv. 24-26a) and destruction (vv. 28-31), which will result in the purification of Zion (vv. 26b-27). The structure of Isaiah 1 can be illustrated in the following manner.

    I. Superscription (v. 1)
   II. The First Speech (vv. 2-9)
       A. The heavens and earth are called "to hear"
  III. The Second Speech (vv. 10-17)
       A. The rulers of Sodom and the people of
          Gemorrah are called "to hear"
  IV. The Third Speech (vv. 18-31)
       A. The inevitability of choice and the offer of grace

This overview illustrates how the present boundaries of the lectionary text have turned an introduction (vv. 18-20) for this section into a conclusion (to vv. 10-17).

Significance. Four points are being made in Isaiah 1:10-20. The first two points are expressed through questions. Verses 11-12 raise the question of why Israel sacrifices (or more generally worships) at all. The way in which the question is posed implies a negative assessment of the cult. The boundaries of this opening unit include:

> What to me is the multitude of your sacrifices?
> . . . .
> When you come to appear before me.

Verses 12*ab*-15*ba* raise a further question about worship. This time it is not a question of why we worship, but who is requiring it? The text reads: "Who asked this from our hand?" The concluding lines of this section make explicit the negative connotations of the questions by confirming the absence of God in worship: "I will hide my eyes from you, even though you make many prayers, I will not listen." The point of these questions is that worship is meaningless for Israel because God is absent. The reason for the divine absence is stated in the third section, which consists of vv. 15*bb*-17. The point of this section is that Israel has bloody hands. They have not extended the character of worship beyond the boundaries of the cult through acts of righteousness and justice. When vv. 18-20 are read as a conclusion to the preceding verses, then the central point to be stressed is the burden of choice on the worshiping community once the fact of divine absence has been revealed to them. Business as usual will inevitably lead to destruction, since worship in God's absence is futile activity (v. 20). Obedience, however, could result in a radical reversal, in which a blood-stained hand would be bleached white. Such activity would go beyond the worshiping community and result in the regeneration of the land.

The central message of Isaiah 1:10-20 is that acts of worship, be they complex services (v. 11), liturgical festivals (v. 14), or individual piety (v. 15) can be occasions of judgment if these activities do not result in transformed behavior outside of the worship setting. The imagery of the text makes the point this way: if God is absent from worship (because of manipulation by the worshipers), then the presence of God outside of it will take the form of destruction. The only hope of reversing such a fate is to claim the presence of God in the cult so that blood can be bleached white. The paradox of Isaiah 1, however, is that the only way to coax God back into the cult is to perform acts of righteousness and justice in the larger community. No amount of prayer, liturgical festivals, or sacrificial acts will help.

The Response: *Psalm 50:1-8, 22-23*

A Theophany of Judgment

Setting. Psalm 50 incorporates much of the imagery of theophany, for it describes an epiphany of God in the setting of worship. The psalm begins by listing three names for God in staccato fashion: Mighty one (Hebrew, *'el*) God (Hebrew, *'elohim*) and Lord (Hebrew, *yhwh*). The location of this theophany is Zion, and it is for the purpose of God to speak a word of judgment to the people of God, who are gathered for worship. Because the emphasis is on speaking, scholars have characterized Psalm 50 as prophetic liturgy. The setting of a prophetic word of judgment to the worshiping community at Zion provides strong and explicit points of contact with Isaiah 1.

Structure. Psalm 50 opens with a description of theophany in vv. 1-6, which provides the setting for two divine speeches, the first in vv. 7-15 ("Hear, O my people, and I will speak."), and the second in vv. 16-22 ("But to the wicked God says"), and a conclusion in v. 23. The larger structure illustrates how the lectionary text includes verses from each section. Yet when vv. 1-8, 22-23 are read together as the lectionary boundaries suggest, they lack coherence. The preacher or worship leader may wish to expand a responsive reading to include larger sections from vv. 7-15 and 16-22.

Significance. The prophetic aspect of Psalm 50 underscores how the epiphany of God is not an end in itself, but leads to a word of judgment. Verse 3 lays the groundwork for linking theophany and judgment, when it states that God does not keep silent. Verses 4-6 call the heavens and earth to witness as God prepares to judge the covenant community. When Psalm 50 is read as a response to Isaiah 1, the emphasis on the judgment of God breaking in to a worshiping community becomes a point of hope. Without such judgment, worship that has degenerated into manipulation is doomed.

New Testament Texts

The epistle reading ponders the nature of faith and its effects on human lives. The Gospel lesson treats the character and necessity of faithfulness. There is no simple or natural connection between the texts, and one may be well advised not to spend time trying to connect the epistle and the Gospel. Both readings, however, are rich in their particular reflections on the basis and constitution of Christian life.

The Epistle: *Hebrews 11:1-3, 8-16*

Faith as the Transformation of Life

Setting. Although Hebrews opens like a treatise, it proceeds like a sermon, and it closes like a letter. The whole of Hebrews is an elaborate discourse on the superiority of Jesus Christ and the meaning of being a person of Christian faith. The whole of Hebrews is written in the tones of a grand exhortation that is designed to encourage the readers to have something more that nominal faith and to live something more than an aimless life. The author works with the stories, characters, and other materials from the Old Testament in formulating an argument designed to explain how Jesus fulfills and exceeds the expectations of Israel while motivating the readers of Hebrews to an active life of faith.

The mention of faith in the last two verses of Hebrews 10 raises the topic of the well-known and beloved reflection on faith in Hebrews 11. The verses of our lesson come in the first half of the entire meditation, so that the verses following our reading continue to present the author's teachings on faith. The epistle reading for this Sunday initially lays a foundation (vv. 1-3) upon which the subsequent materials, both in this reading (vv. 8-16) and the remainder of the chapter (vv. 17-40), continue to build.

Structure. The verses of the reading come from three related sections of the eleventh chapter of Hebrews, an extended meditation on the nature and consequences of faith. The lectionary suggests a beginning with the first verse of this meditation, 11:1, and an ending of the reading after v. 16. By leaving out vv. 4-7 the suggested reading uses vv. 8-16, which begins with a reference to Abraham and ends with a reference to God's heavenly city, as an illustration of the faith that was first declared in vv. 1-3. This reshaping of the text does not abuse Hebrews, for it locates the origins of faith in history and looks forward to God's future as the goal of faith. For the author of Hebrews faith is dynamic, open-ended, and the epistle moves ever forward. After vv. 1-3 the ensuing illustrations move through the history of Israel to show the dynamic character of faith. Thus, Hebrews depicts the linear and progressive qualities of faith; and by having vv. 8-16 follow vv. 1-3, the lectionary moves forward from Abraham and Sarah toward God's better country and heavenly city. Faith presses onward through time toward God.

Significance. The opening verses (1-3) make a statement concerning the nature of faith. This crucial declaration is, however, ambiguous. The author writes, "Faith is the . . . "; and in the Greek text, the word *hypostasis* may mean either "substance" or "assurance" of "the things hoped for." Increasingly translators prefer "assurance" rather than "substance," but in the context of this meditation in Hebrews the older manner of translation ("substance" in KJV) seems preferable.

The author writes of faith as the active life of belief that one sees manifested in the catalogue of heroes of faith that follows throughout 11:4-40. The author is most concerned in chapter 11 with declaring and demonstrating the active nature of faith that produces a life of obedience to the will of God. Indeed this concern is clear, for the author wishes to say that when faith manifests itself in an active, obedient life, the very things for which believers hope become real. Faith produces a life that manifests in the here-and-now the kinds of things that God promises will make up the future. The manifestations of faith in the lives of believers are anticipations of God's future. The substance of faith does not exhaust God's promised future, but it demonstrates its reality. Faith "proves" and "points to" the reality of God's promises. Indeed, faith provides perception of the will and the work of God, as v. 3 states in referring to faith's understanding of creation as the result of God's own creative word.

Having spoken of the nature of faith, Hebrews 11 continues by illustrating the substance of the life of faith as it has been made known in the lives of prominent personalities through Israel's history. Above all, these heroes and heroines show that faith gives the courage to move forward in obedience, even into the unknown. The catalogue of heroes comes in Hebrews 11 in order to encourage the readers to live a robust life of faith. The author's purpose is particularly clear from the manner in which he turns toward the readers to encourage them to Christ-like perseverance in the company or viewing of the host of witnesses discussed in chapter 11 (see 12:1-2). A sermon on this reading that deals with the nature of faith and that calls for vigorous faith that energizes steadfast living will be true to the purposes of this passage.

The Gospel: *Luke 12:32-40*

Living in the Light of God's Love

Setting. As Jesus taught the multitude (12:1), he turned directly to his disciples (12:22) and spoke to them concerning the radical character of discipleship, especially about their assurance of God's love for them. That divine love liberates disciples to devote themselves to God's own purposes. The verses of our lesson build on Jesus' words about assurance and liberation.

Structure. Various Greek and English texts of our lesson suggest an array of ways to divide the verses of the reading into paragraphs. Interpreters debate whether v. 32 should be regarded as the conclusion to Jesus' teachings in 12:22-31 or as the initial comment concerning laying up treasure in heaven in vv. 33-34. While v. 32 seems more thematically coherent with vv. 22-31, it both summarizes and works as a transition to the thoughts of vv. 33-34. In using the text suggested by the lectionary, it is perhaps most helpful to understand that vv. 32-34 and vv. 35-40 are two distinguishable units of Jesus' teaching. Either or both sets of verses may provide the basis of a sermon on the themes of having true concern with God's purposes and the necessity of vigilant readiness for God's final or ultimate act of judgment. The second part of the lesson, vv. 35-40, itself contains two complementary parts: vv. 35-38, a parabolic statement about the value of being ever prepared for God's work; and vv. 39-40, a parabolic declaration about the necessity of being prepared.

Significance. The opening declaration of our lesson tells Jesus' disciples why they are free to live fearlessly according to God's will. God's gracious granting of "the kingdom" is the basis and the standard of the life to which Jesus calls his disciples. Disciples are not told to strive for the kingdom, to achieve it, so that they may live boldly. Rather, Jesus recognizes the priority of God's grace. Because God is pleased to grant Jesus' disciples the kingdom, they are free to live as citizens of that kingdom. What Jesus means by "the kingdom" is clear throughout Luke's Gospel from the words of the Lord's prayer (Luke 11:2-4). The kingdom of God is established by God's own giving of the kingdom. That kingdom is the place where the will of God is actively done. In God's kingdom human needs are met, sinfulness is forgiven, and human beings are transformed so that their own lives model the depths of the love of God (especially in forgiveness), and God directs the very lives of the citizens of his kingdom.

Verses 33-34 are, in part, comparable to Matthew 6:19-21. These lines explicate the life-style of those living according to God's will. Jesus teaches that the lives of his disciples are to be characterized by selfless generosity. In earthly terms one recognizes such living especially in acts of compassion toward those in need, but in spiritual terms Jesus' statement recognizes that one should understand that Christian generosity is an expression of ultimate devotion to God.

The story in vv. 35-38 is somewhat similar in language and theme to the parables found in Matthew 24:45-51 and 25:1-13, although these verses in our lesson from Luke are without a strict parallel. Clearly, however, a central theme of Jesus' teaching was his insistence that his disciples should be watchful and ready for God's decisive action. A key thought in this passage is that humans do not and cannot know the precise time of God's future actions; but they can be absolutely certain that God will act. The mention of the Son of Man picks up the vocabulary and image of Jewish apocalyptic thought, especially as expressed in books such as Daniel. The Son of Man was a more than human heavenly figure who was expected to act at the final cosmic assize as God's agent of judgment. These verses may be read as an indirect threat, but they are more words of promise and assurance that motivate faithfulness than a mere threat. The tone of the teaching is more positive than negative, so in preaching one should work to develop the promise of blessing as the motivation for watchfulness and readiness.

No matter when God acts, those who are prepared will be blessed. In the context of Luke's Gospel, readiness is associated with the life of service and charity discussed in the previous verses. Thus, watchfulness and readiness are the active doing of God's will, not simply waiting around while doing no wrong. The ensuing verses, vv. 39-40, develop this line of thought. Christians have an active job to do as they live in watchful preparation for the coming of God's grand judgment.

Proper 14: The Celebration

Smaller congregations during the height of the summer may allow for some approaches to preaching that may not be practicable during the rest of the year. Laurence A. Wagley, in *Preaching with the Small Congregation* (Nashville: Abingdon Press, 1989), discusses what he calls participatory preaching. This is a method designed to involve the congregation in the body of the sermon and to allow them to suggest the moves the sermon ought to take. Obviously, such a procedure calls for much more preparation by the preacher, since one does not know precisely where the hearers will want to go with the text, but it also allows for an exciting freshness to preaching that respects the ability of the congregation to do theology, and it uses the preacher more as resource than as final authority.

The preacher does need to establish the boundaries of the text or topic for the sermon. Today, for example, the preacher would need to decide which of the lessons is to govern the discussion. If Isaiah, then the opening gambit might involve asking why bother coming to church on such a hot day as this when we could learn to do good and seek justice in more comfortable surroundings. If Hebrews, the preacher might begin by quoting the old axiom that "faith is believing what you know ain't so," and soliciting examples of faithful living in the experience of the congregation. If Luke, the discussion might pursue the meaning of true treasure for Christians.

Limiting the scope of the topic will keep the discussion more manageable and within the time usually allotted for the sermon. The preacher will also be able to use the contributions more effectively in making the final move that closes the sermon. That move may be a general conclusion or primary "point," or it may be a summary of the interpretations that have been offered, each understood as contributing to the church's ongoing dialogue about the significance of the text for the congregation.

Rather than springing this mode of preaching on the congregation, it should be announced a week in advance along with the primary text. People will need to be assured that they do not have to participate orally, but that they should feel free to do so. The pastor will probably know who in the congregation can be counted on to begin the process. This style of preaching calls for a conversational style that makes it important for the preacher to be physically close to the people, not isolated in a pulpit at some distance.

Isaiah can provide today's assurance of pardon:

> Though your sins are like scarlet,
>   they shall be like snow;
> though they are red like crimson,
>   they shall become like wool (1:18*bc*).

and the dismissal at the time of the blessing:

> Learn to do good,
> seek justice,
>   rescue the oppressed,
> defend the orphan,
>   plead for the widow (1:17).

The two following Wesley stanzas can serve as a response to the epistle reading and a preparation for hearing the Gospel reading:

125

Faith, mighty faith, the promise sees,
and looks to that alone,
laughs at impossibilities,
and cries: "It shall be done!"

Obedient faith, that waits on thee,
thou never wilt reprove,
but thou wilt form thy Son in me,
and perfect me in love.
(stanzas 9 and 11 of no. 350 in the 1780 *Collection*)

Use a common meter tune such as Arlington or Azmon.

Proper Fifteen Sunday Between August 14 and 20 Inclusive

Old Testament Texts

Isaiah 5:1-7 is a song about judgment. Psalm 80 is a national lament.

The Lesson: *Isaiah 5:1-7*

The Song of the Vineyard

Setting. Isaiah 5:1-17 has received much attention from commentators because of its form. It appears to be a ballad and this has prompted speculation concerning what kind of context may have produced such a genre. The opening line may provide a partial clue, when the singer is identified as representing a friend, who is a male ("his vineyard"). Some scholars suggest that the singer is a representative of a bridegroom, who is registering a complaint to the bride in a premarriage situation, when custom forbade the bride and groom from communicating directly with each other. But even if this is indeed the situation of the song, it gives way by v. 3 when the groom enters the scene to speak for himself. Thus the song takes on a variety of possible meanings even without the theological interpretation of v. 7. It could be about an owner of land and a vineyard, or about a bride and a bridegroom.

Structure. The shift from a singer representing a friend/groom in vv. 1-2 to the first person speech of the friend/groom in v. 3 provides an initial point of insight for structuring the song. Verses 1-2 represent the ballad, which give way to direct speeches in vv. 3-6. These speeches divide further between vv. 3-4 and 5-6. Note how

127

both units begin with the phrase, "And now . . . ." Verse 7 is either the ballad singer of vv. 1-2 or an additional prophetic voice. In either case this verse functions as a theological interpretation of the preceding unit by identifying the owner of the vineyard/groom as Yahweh and the vineyard/bride as Israel, which provides yet another reading to the song.

Another structure is also evident in Isaiah 5:1-7 and it will provide the key for interpretation. The song is meant to resemble a judgment speech with legal connotations, in which accusations, complaints, and judgment are assigned. Verses 1-2 present a situation somewhat impersonally, which lays out the accusations of the friend/owner/groom. A third party tells how there was a person who owned a fertile plot of land, cleared it, planted it, watched over it; but in the end it yielded wild grapes. The speech becomes more immediate and personal in vv. 3-4 for three reasons: the ballad singer is replaced by the friend/owner/groom; the indefinite past time of the opening story is pulled into the present time ("And now"); and the audience is made the jury. The result of these shifts in speaker, role of audience, and time is that the accusations of vv. 1-2 are made more sharply by calling the present audience to witness. Verses 5-6, however, do not present the response of the audience/witness/jury. Instead the friend/owner/groom jumps in to provide the judgment. The vineyard will be destroyed and the land will be allowed to lie fallow.

Significance. For preaching it is important to see that there is no real choice by the audience in the song of the vineyard. It is not a confrontation demanding a decision, as was the case last week in Isaiah 1:10-20 (especially in vv. 18-20). Instead, the song of the vineyard is an indictment and judgment after choices have been made. The vineyard has already yielded bad grapes, the only decision left is by the owner/spouse concerning what should now be done with the bad investment. Several aspects of the context and the language of Isaiah 5:1-7 illustrate the finality of this song. First, it is important to see that Isaiah 5:1-7 is meant to function as the conclusion to the first five chapters of Isaiah. Chapter 1 introduced judgment oracles along with warnings, which laid out the consequences of choice. Chapters 2–4 have consisted primarily of oracles of judgment concerning social abuse. These chapters functioned as the time of pruning. The song of the vineyard simply underscores the failure of Israel. Second, the theological interpretation in v. 7 is also about the end result of a process. This message is carried through by two word plays. God looked for justice *(mišpat)* but received bloodshed *(mispah)*, for righteousness *(ṣedaqah)* but found a cry *(ṣeaqah)*. Third, the song provides the introduction for a series of woe oracles in Isaiah 5:8-30, which are meant to fill out the content of the judgment. And, finally, a quick look at the prophet's call in 6:1-13 will underscore how the content of this call is not to bring Israel back to God, but simply to confirm blindness in the people (vv. 9-13). The song of the vineyard is a chilling text to preach. It underscores how there are *kairos* moments, which when they pass, have the potential of sealing our fate. This is not a text about an arbitrary God. It is a text about immoral people.

The Response: *Psalm 80:1-2, 8-19*

A Prayer for Salvation

Setting. Psalm 80 is a national lament in which the community of faith is pictured as waiting for the salvation of God and as calling upon God to bring about a new salvation. Some scholars describe the genre of Psalm 80 as a community prayer song instead of a national lament, because of the use of the phrase *people's prayer* in v. 4. The implied situation of a community prayer, however, is similar to that of a national lament in that it, too, presupposes a time of distress.

Structure. The lectionary reading consists primarily of the second half of a large psalm, the whole of which can be outlined in four parts.

    I. A Plea for Help (vv. 1-3)
    II. A Description of Divine Anger (vv. 4-7)
    III. A Recounting of Past Salvation (vv. 8-13)
    IV. A Plea for Help (vv. 14-19)

Woven throughout the psalm is the refrain, "Restore us, O God; / let your face shine, that we may be saved" (vv. 3, 7, 19). The liturgist may wish to expand the lectionary reading to vv. 1-3, 8-19 in order to include this refrain in the opening verses of the psalm.

Significance. The refrains in vv. 3 and 19 provide the central theme for interpreting Psalm 80:1-2, 8-19. God is absent and the community undertakes a sustained effort to invoke God to return, so that they might be saved. This call for salvation goes beyond the finality of Isaiah 5:1-7, even while vv. 8-19 pick up many of the images of the vineyard.

New Testament Texts

Hebrews urges its readers to focused persistence along the path of faith. The verses of our reading praise Jesus Christ as "the pioneer and perfecter of our faith," as they present him as the very mark toward which Christians press onward in life. The verses from Luke recognize the controversial nature of Jesus' person and work and move to confront us with our failure to recognize the situation in which we find ourselves because of who Jesus is and what he does.

The Epistle: *Hebrews 11:29–12:2*

Looking to Jesus and Running with Perseverance

Setting. The book of Hebrews divides into major sections, which meditate on crucial Old Testament texts in order to provide guidance for Christian living. The fourth major section of Hebrews is 10:19–12:29. Here one finds an exposition of the new and living way of Christian covenantal life. The author develops the dynamic concept of faith prominently in this section, working out a linear scheme that shows the necessity of growth, progress, and action in the lives of believers. The author employs images from Exodus 19, Deuteronomy 4, Genesis 4, perhaps even Enoch 22, and a quotation from Deuteronomy 9 to warn and urge the readers to accept God's grace.

Structure. Hebrews 11:29-39 continues a celebration of faithful Israelites (many were martyrs), who preceded Jesus in doing God's will. It continues with the litany of examples who acted out the drama of Israelite history "by faith." And yet their faith, however noble, was not enough to benefit from the promise of perfect faith, which can only be found in the courage of Jesus. Verses 1-2 are a challenging call to courageous commitment to the struggles of faithful living. The lines of the lesson present these themes: the context of the Christian calling (v. 1) and the christologically formed standard and goal of faith (v. 2). In a sense, the momentum of the lesson takes the matter of Christian calling through the dimensions of comfort, challenge, and assurance.

Significance. The author operates with the assumption that his readers are facing discouraging difficulties specifically because of their Christian identity. He opens chapter 12 with a reference to the great cloud of witnesses who surround the readers. These witnesses are the men and women whose faith-stories were chronicled through chapter 11. Having told these stories from the past, the author shifts to focus on the Christians in his own time and refers to the faithful people who have gone before them as a word of encouragement. Notice that the encouragement is not a threat of embarrassment. The witnesses are examples, or better, they are testimony to the reality of faithfulness; they are not spectators or judges watching and monitoring the performance of the readers. The readers are to look to the witnesses who are proof of the reality of a life of full devotion to God. The witnesses have lived the reality to which the author calls his readers, and because their lives testify to the reality of faithfulness, they are in themselves witnesses.

The supreme one to whom the readers are to look, however, is Jesus himself. Above all, his life of faithful devotion and obedience is proof of the reality to which the readers are called. Thus, his story is the supreme encouragement to which the author calls the attention of the readers. Calling the readers to meditate on Jesus Christ directs their attention away from a mere focus on themselves and the probable hardships that they face. As the readers focus on Jesus—seeing his faithfulness despite the shame of the cross and seeing how God richly honored him—they can, in turn, reevaluate their own situation(s) knowing that "for the sake of the joy that [is] set before [them]" they are able to press on in faithfulness to God. Whatever comes their way, the readers of Hebrews know through God's work in Jesus Christ that their own faithfulness is grounded in the faithfulness of Jesus Christ and God. Because God is faithful, we are assured that we may live faithfully.

131

The Gospel: *Luke 12:49-56*

Jesus Causes Division That Demands Discernment

Setting. As we follow Luke's account of Jesus' journey to Jerusalem, which began at 9:51 and continues through 19:27, we move through a series of three major sections of the story (9:51–13:21; 13:22–17:10; 17:11–19:27). Each section is thematically unified although the larger blocks of material have several subsections. Our lesson comes in the first major section, which is concerned with discipleship and mission.

Structure. Despite the paragraphing of the NRSV and other recent translations, the verses of the lesson compose three distinct "sayings" of Jesus. First, vv. 49-50 strike an apocalyptic note as they speak in metaphors of fire and baptism concerning both Jesus' purpose in ministry and his anticipation of completing the work to which he understood himself to be directed. Second, the apocalyptic tone continues in vv. 51-55 as Jesus tells of the critical separation that comes because of his work. These first two sections are directed to the disciples, but a turn occurs in the account as Jesus next speaks to the multitudes. In the third element of our lesson, vv. 54-56, Jesus confronts the crowd, contrasting their capacity to forecast the weather from current conditions with their inability to look at the present course of life and, thus, to anticipate God's future. Jesus' dedication and earnest desire to do God's will, the critical and demanding character of his work, and the crisis brought upon humanity by Jesus' presence and work are the major themes of the lesson. The lesson moves from Christology through human crisis to confrontation and demand. The logic of the sermon may profitably follow the course of the lesson, although the single theme of either of the three subsections could inform more coherent, though less dynamic, proclamation.

Significance. Two portions of our lesson, vv. 51-53 and 54-56, are comparable to Matthew 10:34-36 and Matthew 16:2-3, respectively. These two segments of five total verses probably belonged to a common source available to Luke and Matthew, so that comparison of the lines in Luke and Matthew is helpful for grasping the special focus of the lines in our lesson.

The first segment of our lesson, vv. 49-50, however, is without parallel. Here Jesus tells his disciples that the purpose of his coming forth in ministry is analogous to putting a torch to the face of the earth. The references to baptism in the ensuing parallel statement heighten the eschatological character of the time and the eschatological nature of Jesus' ministry. These metaphorical pronouncements highlight the crucial nature of both Jesus' preaching and Passion. As Jesus lives and teaches in Luke we learn that his appearance and proclamation produced a crisis, first in Israel and, then, among all humanity. As Jesus embodies, proclaims, and calls others to God's ways, he evokes both a following and harsh rejection. Thus, we see God effecting a judgment among humans, separating those aligned with God and willing to do God's will from those opposed to God and set in opposition to God's grace, mercy, justice, and love. In vv. 49-50 Jesus states his eagerness to establish God's judgment and his anxiety as he looks devotedly, but with dread, toward the price he will pay for demanding that God's will be done—namely, his suffering and death.

Verses 51-53 magnify the reality of division brought by Jesus' ministry. Through comparison to Matthew's version of this saying it is clear that Micah 7:6 provided the basis for Jesus' statement here about divisions in families. The strife that Jesus' call to doing God's will brings is illustrated dramatically in the opposition portrayed among members of families toward one another. This set of statements is both traditional and hyperbolic, but it may be (and, in fact, has been) actual. Persons who hear and respond to Christ's call to labor for justice in society often find themselves misunderstood and even rejected by members of their own families. The point is that when one hears Jesus' call there is no possibility of neutrality: one either does or rejects God's will as Jesus presents it. Coming after the metaphorical reference to Jesus' Passion we should see that "taking sides" with Jesus may cause suffering.

The final portion of our lesson may not require meteorological expertise, but many modern readers or hearers of this saying may be so thoroughly urbanized that the references to weather make little sense. If the preacher does not get what Jesus is talking about, he or she should turn to critical commentaries for an explanation (taking for granted that often urbanized commentators have bothered to educate themselves about the "plain" sense of the text).

Remarkably, Matthew and Luke present different versions of the saying. Perhaps Jesus of Nazareth spoke on several occasions about the weather, using that topic as a point of departure for commenting on the ridiculous human failure to discern God's will. More likely, early Christians knew different versions of what Jesus said, although the "point" is always the same. Humans learn to read the weather. They see its patterns and learn its ways. But humans do not apply themselves with equal fervor to learning, discerning, and living with or according to God's will, which is certainly more regular than the weather. In the church today there are Christians who are extremely sophisticated readers of economic and political trends: they know exactly how to play the stock market or exactly how to use voters' opinions to their favor. But, by contrast, these same persons demonstrate minimal ability to think theologically about the crucial issues of life. Jesus identifies such inexcusable behavior and demands a better showing.

Proper 15: The Celebration

Before tackling either the Old Testament lesson or Jesus' words in the Gospel reading about bringing fire upon the earth, preachers need to be clear about what they mean by the wrath or judgment of God and its place in their systematic theology. It is first important to distinguish between the personal and impersonal wrath of God. In the Old Testament, the wrath of God is usually personal; God has been offended in some way, as by the neglect of justice in today's lesson, and God therefore becomes angry and exacts retribution upon the offender. In the New Testament, the wrath of God is described in more impersonal terms; God is never referred to as being angry. The "wrath of God" has more to do with the human condition as subject to sin than with a divine emotion, but the Church in its preaching has not always been careful to respect the difference. The result has been doctrines that place humanity in total enmity to God and that understand redemption only in terms of Christ receiving the full force of God's anger. And preachers have been all too ready to identify their own personal wrath with that of God. As Anthony Trollope complained:

With what complacency will a young parson deduce false conclusion from misunderstood texts, and then threaten us with all the penalties of Hades if we neglect to comply with the injunctions he has given us! Yes, my too self-confident juvenile friend, I do believe in those mysteries, which are so common in your mouth; I do believe in the unadulterated word which you hold there in your hand; but you must pardon me if, in some things, I doubt your interpretation.

> Anthony Trollope, *Barchester Towers, and The Warden*
> (New York: Modern Library, 1950), p. 252

A set of lessons such as we have today indicates how questionable it is to talk about *a* biblical theology. What the Bible contains is a variety of theologies that the preacher needs to continually compare and synthesize. Any literal reading of the Old Testament about the wrath of God leaves one in the hands of a very capricious divinity. As A. T. Hanson put it, we need the New Testament's demythologizing of the Old Testament so that the wrath of God can be understood as the consequences of sin "working themselves out in society through the ages." That is why the sins of the parents are visited upon the children—for example, why the miracle of fluorocarbons in the 30s becomes the misery of skin cancer with the depletion of the ozone layer in the 90s. *Sin* in the New Testament sense of the term is simply too complicated for human beings to do anything about. Christ's redemptive suffering offends our human standards of justice and so brings division between those who submit to grace and those who seek to earn it. Christ pioneers for us a new citizenship, a new relationship wherein the consequences of sin become a ladder to redemption.

The following Wesley stanza, sung to St. George's Windsor, may serve as a response to the Gospel reading.

> See how great a flame aspires,
> kindled by a spark of grace.
> Jesus' love the nations fires,
> sets the kingdoms on a blaze.
> To bring fire on earth he came,
> kindled in some hearts it is;
> O that all might catch the flame,
> all partake the glorious bliss!

> (*The United Methodist Hymnal*, 1989, no. 541)

Proper Sixteen
Sunday Between August
21 and 27 Inclusive

Old Testament Texts

Jeremiah 1:4-10 is the call of the prophet Jeremiah. Psalm 71:1-6 is a prayer of trust.

The Lesson: *Jeremiah 1:4-10*

A Prophetic Commission During Chaotic Times

Setting. Jeremiah 1:4-10 fits into the category of a call narrative (for a detailed discussion of this form see Year A, Proper 17). The term *call narrative* is used to describe how certain individuals are confronted by God to function in a specific task. Moses, for example, is called specifically to save Israel by leading them from Egypt (Exodus 3). Gideon, on the other hand, must rescue the Israelites from the Midianites (Judges 6). In *Jeremiah, A Commentary* (in The Old Testament Library [Louisville: Westminster John Knox, 1986]) Robert P. Carroll has noted the very concrete tasks that tend to characterize call narratives, and, in view of this, he suggests that such texts might better be characterized as commissions rather than calls, since the word *call* tends to be a more abstract category about ordination. Commissions, on the other hand, concern a specific task by a specific person or group of persons for a specific time. A special priestly or prophetic office is neither implied in the commission nor does ordination necessarily follow. Gideon provides a biblical example of this distinction, when he explicitly refuses to accept an office of leadership after his task is finished.

Furthermore, because of the specific nature of the task in a call or a commission narrative, the confrontation between God and the designated person also tends to be very concrete. Moses is tending sheep when God addresses him from the burning bush, while Gideon is pounding out grain. These two examples illustrate how the commission itself tends to be rooted in mundane experience, so that it can be recounted by the one being called. The distinction between a call and a commission provides important background for interpreting Jeremiah 1:4-10. This text falls clearly into the category of a commission, which suggests that the call takes place at a specific time and includes a specific assignment. Yet the imagery of the call works against the reader's expectations. Instead of a call that could be anchored in Jeremiah's daily routine so that it might be recounted at a later date, he tells us that God called him to his task in his mother's uterus. The imagery here goes against the very character of a commission. What can this possibly mean for interpreting the commission of Jeremiah?

Structure. Jeremiah 1:4-10 has many of the parts of the call narrative, but the order is not clear. One way to read these verses is to follow the expected sequence of a call narrative: commission (v. 5), objection (v. 6), reassurance (vv. 7-8), and sign (v. 9). But there are problems with this reading. The most central is that v. 5 lacks the verb "to send" (Hebrew, *slh*) which tends to be a formulaic element in commissions. It does occur, however, in v. 7, which suggests that perhaps this verse is meant to be the commission, resulting in the following structure: an introductory word (v. 5), objection (v. 6), commission (v. 7), reassurance (v. 8), and sign with a summary statement (vv. 9-10).

Significance. The career of Jeremiah took place during one of the most chaotic times in the history of ancient Israel. International political structures were collapsing around Judah—which, in turn, were challenging established social and religious beliefs. In short, it was a time when the mere repetition of orthodoxy was inadequate, and the call of Jeremiah in 1:4-10 has been constructed in such a way as to alert us to this fact. It is a text that couldn't exist without tradition, since it presupposes the standard form of commission, even though it is critical of it. Tradition is criticized in three ways: First, there is no clear-cut occasion for the confrontation between God and Jeremiah. Second, Jeremiah is never given a choice about participating in the divine commission. And, third, the specific content of the commission is unclear. An examination of v. 5 and the structure of Jeremiah's call will illustrate these points.

First, the blurring of a real occasion for the confrontation between God and Jeremiah. Although v. 5 clearly describes a confrontation (or perhaps better an introductory word) between God and Jeremiah, the prenatal imagery is hardly the setting that one expects for such a confrontation. Scholars have noted how the claim of divine commission prior to one's birth has parallels in ancient Near Eastern royal declarations. See, for example, the address of the Egyptian god Amun to king Painchi, where the god informs the king that he was called to rule already when he was in the belly of his mother. This parallel suggests that there may be royal imagery influencing the call of Jeremiah, but such an analogy does not account for the drastic change in Jeremiah 1:4-10, since such a commission from the womb is unparalleled in the prophetic calls. Another line of interpretation is to emphasize how the language of v. 5 eliminates any real choice on the part of the prophet with regard to his commission by removing the point of origin from his life experience. Twice the word *before* is used (Hebrew, *btrm*) to emphasize the passive state of Jeremiah with regard to divine activity ("before I formed you," and "before you were born"). In addition, three divine actions toward Jeremiah are described in his birth process, which suggest a progression from conception (God knew [Hebrew, *yd'*] him in the womb), through the labor of his birth (God sanctified [Hebrew, *qds*] him from the womb), to his prophetic career (God made [Hebrew, *ntn*] him a prophet to the nations). The choice of verbs reinforces Jeremiah's lack of active participation in his commission, especially the Hebrew verb *yd'*, with its sexual connotations of conception, and *qds*, which suggests a divine claim on Jeremiah already at his birth through its root meaning of being set apart.

Second, the structure of Jeremiah 1:4-10. Interpretation of v. 5 has followed the second outline noted above, in which this verse is read as an introductory word rather than a commission. Such an interpretation of the larger structure of Jeremiah 1:4-10 reinforces further the passivity of Jeremiah, since the introductory word already sketches out his entire career. In view of this situation it is understandable that Jeremiah's first response in v. 6 is an objection, but we should note that it is out of place from the expected form, since the commission does not really come until the following verse. Jeremiah's objection in v. 7, that he is too young and that he does not know (Hebrew, *yd'*) how to speak, are his only words in the text, and they are strongly silenced by God ("Do not say, 'I am only a boy' "), before divine speech takes over for the remainder of the text with a commission (v. 7*b*), reassurance (v. 8), and a sign (v. 9). The structure of Jeremiah's commission reinforces the interpretation of v. 5, that the prophet has no real choice in accepting the divine call.

The interrelationship of three themes, in particular, will provide a point of departure for preaching. First and foremost, the call of Jeremiah provides an example of a divine commission that does not arise from any kind of prophetic experience. There is no concrete occasion that the prophet can recount to validate his task, which is required by the call form. This fact places Jeremiah in a critical relationship with his tradition. Second, in the absence of specific experience to validate his commission, the prophet turns to images of conception and birth to argue that the word of God has simply been implanted in him, and that because of this he has no choice but to speak it. Once again, such vague criteria puts the prophet in tension with the orthodox requirements of tradition to validate a commission with more specific experience. And, third, the vagueness of his commission is carried over into his task. What exactly does it mean to be a prophet to the nations and how would either he or his hearers know when the task was accomplished? These three themes combine to underscore the ambiguity of Jeremiah's commission. He goes through the expected processes of a call, yet the prenatal context and the rearranging of the order of the text call into question the very orthodoxy of the call process. The prophet's commission is neither anchored in a clear occasion, nor is he given any real choice about whether to accept or reject the call.

The end result of using a traditional call form to introduce Jeremiah, even while its meaning is blurred, is that the prophet is presented as an archetype of how the people of God live during ambiguous or chaotic times, when the simple repetition of orthodox answers itself becomes part of the problem rather than the solution.

And it is at this point that the call of Jeremiah mirrors a problem that presently plagues the contemporary church, which like this text couldn't exist without tradition even though it is critical of it. Here the call of Jeremiah provides more than an analogous situation to become itself authoritative tradition, because it provides guidelines for action in such unsure times, one of which is that we simply keep talking about the faith even when the source of authority, the concrete task of a commission, and its outcome might be unclear. In such a situation the mere act of speaking (of which worship is one form) may provide the link to a new formulation of tradition.

The Response: *Psalm 71:1-6*

A Prayer of Trust

Setting. Psalm 71 contains a variety of traditional elements, which make it difficult to classify. It begins with the language of asylum in v. 1*b* ("In you, O LORD, I take refuge"), which is used by persons taking refuge in the sanctuary. The psalm may thus be classified as a lament, in which the worshiper also demonstrates a strong trust that God is able to save.

Structure. The lectionary reading is limited to vv. 1-6, which could be divided into a section of petition (vv. 1-3) and praise (4-6). Each half begins with a petition that God rescue the psalmist. The difference between the two sections is that the second introduces language of trust and praise. These sections would most likely divide differently if the entire psalm were being considered and the reader is encouraged to consult the commentaries for an interpretation of the entire psalm.

Significance. The imagery of the psalmist having been taken by God from his mother's womb provides a strong point of contact with the call of Jeremiah. This similar imagery, along with the language of petition and especially trust allows the psalm to become an extension of the call of Jeremiah for the worshiping community.

New Testament Texts

Hebrews presents Jesus Christ as "the mediator of a new covenant" and, after creating a crucial christological focus, calls the readers to faithfulness. From this focus the text calls the readers to a deeper appreciation of what God has done for them in the covenant of grace in Jesus Christ. The Gospel lesson tells the story of Jesus' administering healing grace to a woman on the Sabbath. This seemingly scandalous activity created a controversy and presented an opportunity for Jesus to declare that God wills human wholeness twenty-four hours a day, seven days a week. Humans are to act accordingly.

The Epistle: *Hebrews 12:18-29*

Looking to Jesus, the Mediator of a New Covenant, and to God, Our Gracious Judge

Setting. The verses come again from the fourth major section of Hebrews (10:19–12:29). Readers may consult the discussion of setting for last week's epistle reading for fuller information about this part of Hebrews.

Structure. The verses of the lesson present these themes: the terrifying and impossible holiness of the first covenant (vv. 18-21), the gracious beauty and fellowship with angels, saints, God, and Jesus in the context of the new covenant (vv. 22-24), and a vivid word of warning against rejecting God's grace (vv. 25-29). Thus, the lesson takes readers through the themes of awful holiness, the beauty of grace, and the possible danger of refusing grace.

Significance. The author operates with the assumption that his readers are facing discouraging difficulties specifically because of their Christian identity. Perhaps in an effort to discourage the threat of possible nostalgia for a former religious life without the hardships of Christian identity, the author recalls the terrible holy otherness of the relationship of people to God in the life of the first covenant. The images in vv. 18-21 encourage appreciation for participation in the new covenant by recalling the frightening, even threatening conditions of the first covenant.

In comparison with the first covenant vv. 22-24 portray the serene beauty of the new covenant. The images abound, but notice that the readers are reminded that in the context of the new covenant they enjoy a rich cluster of relationships—with angels, saints, God, and

Jesus. Whether the author ordered this list of relations in a deliberate sequence is uncertain. But he certainly understands that it is through a relationship to Jesus, "the mediator of a new covenant," that they enjoy their new relationship to God, "the judge of all"; and because God is judge of all, the readers are, in turn, related to "the assembly of the firstborn who are enrolled in heaven." Because of the heavenly setting of that congregation the readers also have a relationship with "innumerable angels in festal gathering." Notice especially how Jesus once again emerges in a key position in the author's understanding of the meaning of the new covenant.

Having contrasted the old and the new covenants, the author raises the real and disturbing possibility that the readers could refuse to hear God's offer of grace. This terrible possibility exists because it is possible that the reader could actually reject God's grace. They could attempt to hold onto the old covenant, or they could attempt to return to that covenant—thus dismissing or rejecting the new covenant of grace. Hebrews says bluntly that there is no holding on to or returning to the previous covenant. The readers will find their relationship to God granted in God's grace or they will experience God's terrible judgment. Hebrews calls the readers away from looking backward to what went before (the old covenant) and calls them to look to the present and the future as God's good and gracious gift (the new covenant).

Few Christians today struggle with an urge to return to Judaism, especially to the practice of Temple piety. Thus, the negative dimensions of the reading find little relevance in the life of contemporary congregations. The sermon will do well to sing the praises of God's new covenant in Jesus Christ, but there is no profit in lambasting the previous covenant.

The Gospel: *Luke 13:10-17*

Doing God's Work in God's Good Time

Setting. As Jesus continued to wind his way toward Jerusalem Luke tells of his teaching one Sabbath in a synagogue. In that setting Jesus performed a controversial healing, which brought him into direct confrontation with the ruler of the synagogue. The synagogue setting heightens the conflict, for as Jesus works in a clearly religious context he violates the religious sensibilities of the members of the religious status quo. Accordingly his final confronting words pronounce God's judgment on the genuinely religious, who manifest an unimaginative, unloving, rigid religiosity all too characteristic of persons more intent on following the letter of the law than on recognizing God's will and looking for every possible opportunity to live in compliance with that will. Humanly constructed regulations, rather than divinely revealed purposes, are not to direct life. Yes, God calls for Sabbath observance, but not in indifference to God's own concerns.

Structure. Luke initially locates Jesus and the woman in the synagogue where Jesus was teaching and, then, the structure of the account unfolds in action (Jesus heals the woman, vv. 12-13), reaction (the synagogue ruler objects and informs Jesus how he ought to behave, v. 14), confrontation or rebuttal (Jesus declares the hypocrisy and inadequacy of the ruler's position, vv. 15-16), and results (the opponents are shamed and the people rejoice at Jesus' work, v. 17). Constructive preaching from this text should work more to help hearers comprehend the shameful failure of rigid religion (and to move beyond it) than to confront the congregation's own patterns of religious inflexibility in an effort to shame the listeners.

Significance. As the story opens there is no sign that tension existed in the synagogue as Jesus taught. The most radical words often go without reaction until they are made real through action. Thus, as Jesus turns to the woman, we find the opening of the controversy. Luke informs us that the woman had suffered for eighteen years. Whatever her problem (medical diagnosis of her condition is sheer speculation) we are to understand that the suffering was severe and extensive. Whether Luke would have the readers understand that this woman was bent from the oppressive insensitivity of the religious leaders is impossible to determine, although the homiletical imagination is not simply unbridled by such observation. As a woman this character was in a kind of double-jeopardy; cattle were more important than women in segments of ancient Palestinian culture.

Jesus himself interprets the affliction in terms of Satan's binding the woman, so that we should see this healing as a vaguely portrayed

143

exorcism. In this instance Jesus applies God's power to a human life in order to break the bonds placed upon that life by the very real forces of evil. Jesus' healing touch brings freedom from the forces that oppressed this woman's essential human existence. Jesus' seemingly spontaneous reaction to seeing this woman models the kind of compassionate action to which a genuine relation to God should direct our lives. God's love never merely plays by the rules of formal religion; what is regular and predictable about God's love is that it always occurs naturally, not by mere prescription. Rules do not regulate God.

The woman's response to being healed also models the shape of the experience of grace—she praised God. The woman recognized the true source of liberation to be God. Indeed, real freedom from the oppressing forces of evil is the work of God alone, though as God worked in this instance through Jesus, God continues to work in the world through humans whom God elects to be agents of divine grace.

By contrast the ruler of the synagogue is scandalized by the healing. According to this man, freedom from Satan's bondage is great, but only on certain days of the week. In other words, there are times to do God's work, but there are times not to do it. For this man, devotion to God means recognizing the time not to do God's work. Incredibly, the time not to do God's work is the time one sets apart for relating to God. At its core this kind of thinking is rotten, but the ruler makes sure the crowd gets his point, so that they are not "misled" by the seemingly too-liberal Jesus who apparently does not know the rules of status quo religion.

When Jesus speaks he talks to the assembly in the synagogue, "You hypocrites!" Ever smooth and sensitive this Jesus, or is he? Jesus argues from a lesser to a greater truth. The rigidly religious recognize the necessity to make basic provisions for their livestock on the Sabbath, but confronted with human bondage to the forces of evil, in the name of God, they do no good on the day they claim to have devoted to God. As Jesus speaks he refers to the woman as "a daughter of Abraham," thus recalling God's initiative toward forming the covenant with Israel. God's will, not a set of rules, is to govern the lives of those whom God has called out in grace. To experience grace means we are to live graciously, at all times and in every possible way.

The shame of rigid religion is that in God's name it often does no good, and so it does real harm. But when God's grace is seen in action, we find ourselves filled with joy in response to the true glory of God. The world sees God's grace in the compassion we display in God's name, not in our merely following a set of religious rules.

Proper 16: The Celebration

Today's Gospel reading provides an occasion to help the congregation distinguish between the Sabbath and the Lord's Day, since in many places it is still customary to refer to Sunday as the Sabbath and to impose on it the kind of rigorous observance that is dictated in the Ten Commandments. The sabbatarianizing of Sunday is one evidence of how conformity to religious rules is more popular than the responsibility given by freedom in Christ.

On the other hand, an exercise of freedom by some congregations to adjust the times of worship to the convenience of their membership can begin to blur the significance of the first day of the week as a temporal symbol that reminds us of God's actions in creation, redemption, and sanctification. Saturday evening services, which are becoming very popular in some sections of the country, serve to remind us of our spiritual roots in Judaism, where the new day begins at sundown. Following that pattern, the first service of the Lord's Day would be Saturday night. While it is commendable to provide a service during the week for those families away on weekends, it is still important to stress the symbolic function of Sunday for Christian worship and to encourage families to include Sunday worship in their travel and vacation plans wherever they are. The Church becomes less than catholic when people begin to feel that they have not worshiped each week if they have not done so in their own parish church. Vacation can be a time for families to discover the diversity that exists within their own denomination and Christianity generally as they take advantage of church services in a range of communities and settings.

This raises the question of the ministry of hospitality to be exercised by churches when they have visitors. One finds everything from total neglect to suffocating embrace. Hospitality begins with an inviting exterior that clearly marks access to the sanctuary and lists service times on a bulletin board large enough so that those "who run may read." A church that alters its entrance to the side away from the street and posts no signs designating the new entrance is saying that only those in the know are welcome. The same is true when service times change in the summer, but the notice board doesn't. Visitors, once inside, should be made to feel at ease and comfortable, but they should not have the spotlight cast upon them willy-nilly. While some persons may enjoy running a gauntlet of goodwill by standing and introducing themselves, others may shy away from such an interruption of their worship, and their feelings also need to be respected. A job of ushers in large churches should be to see that visitors have the necessary tools to do the work of worship (usually a bulletin and hymnal) and that it is clear how to use them. In smaller churches, where visitors or strangers are probably more immediately recognized, it is the ministry of all the membership to assist newcomers in feeling at ease in the service without subjecting them to interrogation. In the service itself, usually a general word of welcome is sufficient. An invitation to remain for a social time after the service then allows the visitors to exercise initiative as to how much "fellowshiping" they wish to do and how soon.

August 28, which this Sunday will fall near, is the feast day of St. Augustine of Hippo, author of a classical Christian interpretation of history, *The City of God*, which draws in part upon today's epistle lesson for its vision of the end of history. It is from his more popularly known *Confessions* that the following has been adapted for use as an opening prayer.

> You are great, O Lord, and greatly to be praised.
> Great is your power, and your wisdom is infinite.
> We desire to praise you:
>> we, a part of your creation;
>> we, who are mortal creatures,
>>> subject to sin and death
>>> because of our sinful pride.

Yet we desire to praise you
because we are a part of your creation.
You have made us find delight in praising you;
for you have made us for yourself
and our hearts are restless till they find rest in you.

Suggested sermon hymns for today are:
  Old Testament: "Praise to the Lord, the Almighty"
  Epistle: "Come, Ye that Love the Lord"
  Gospel: "There's a Wideness in God's Mercy"

Proper Seventeen
Sunday Between August 28 and September 3 Inclusive

Old Testament Texts

Jeremiah 2:4-13 is a disputation speech by God against Israel. Psalm 81 continues the style of prophetic discourse from Jeremiah 2 with further recounting of Israel's disobedience and a call for Israel to return to faithfulness.

The Lesson: *Jeremiah 2:4-13*

Asking the Right Questions

Setting. Jeremiah 2 begins a section of judgment oracles that continues at least through 4:4, if not all the way through chapter 6. Jeremiah 2 begins with two separate messenger formulas, "Thus says the LORD." The first occurs in v. 1 and the second in v. 4. This repetition suggests that Jeremiah 2 has been fashioned into two separate oracles, vv. 1-3 and 4-37 or 3:5. The opening oracle recounts an idyllic time in the past between Israel and God with the metaphor of marriage. Early in the marriage, when Israel was a new bride in the wilderness, she was faithful to God. This pure setting in the wilderness provides contrast (and hence evidence against Israel) to the action of the people once they entered the land. The second oracle beginning with vv. 4-5 addresses the breakdown of the marriage and probes the reasons for it. The lectionary text includes only the opening sections of this more extended oracle. Yet the boundaries of the text make clear that God has entered into a disputation with Israel. This disputation is probably best read within the context of the family and marriage rather than in the larger and more legal context of covenant law. Implicit in the marriage metaphor is the relationship between God and the people of God in the setting of worship. The question arises as to just what Israel has done in the land (and more specifically in worship) that has prompted God to pursue divorce proceedings against the people.

Structure. The first clue to the structure of the text is the opening messenger formula in vv. 4-5. The central question for structuring the text concerns how far the oracle is meant to continue in the present form of the book. A quick look at one repetitive motif in particular suggests that vv. 4-5 continue through 3:5. The motif is the repeated quotation by God of what Israel or her leaders either said or failed to say:

> v. 6: They did not say . . .
> v. 8: The priests did not say . . .
> v. 20: And you said, "I will not serve!"
> v. 23: How can you say, "I am not defiled . . ."
> v. 27: Who say to a tree, "You are my father,"

But in the time of their trouble they say, "Come and save us!"

> v. 31: Why then do my people say, "We are free . . ."
> v. 35: You say, "I am innocent . . ."
> 3:1, Saying . . . (This important linking word is
> eliminated in the NRSV translation).

An overview of the nine instances in which God presents evidence in the disputation through quotation brings to light how the first two references in vv. 6, 8 are not about something that Israel said, but about something that they failed to say. Once this failure of asking the proper questions or of making the proper inquiry is noted, then the remainder of the "sayings" becomes illustrations of improper statements or claims, which provide illustrations of guilt or blindness in the people. Thus, the lectionary text in vv. 4-13 is about the failure of asking the proper questions. The text would separate into two distinct units, vv. 4-9 and 10-13. Verses 4-9 appear to be a judgment oracle introduced by the messenger formula (vv. 4-5) followed by two sections of accusation (vv. 6-7 and 8), which culminate in a judgment signaled by the word "therefore" (v. 9). Yet no judgment is given in v. 9. Instead accusation continues, "Therefore once more I accuse you, and I accuse your children's children." Verses 10-13 function as additional evidence, which culminates in the citing of two evils in v. 13 that are the result of Israel's inability to ask the proper question.

Significance. The larger context of 2:1-3 is important for interpreting vv. 4-13, since these previous verses underscore how the lectionary text is addressed to people with a long and established relationship between themselves and God. What this indicates is that the intended audience is the established people of God, who believe in and maintain the central religious traditions. Their long and fixed relationship with God makes the assertions of vv. 4-13 startling, namely that once Israel was in the land neither the past ancestors nor the present leaders asked, "Where is the Lord?" The problem that is being addressed in the text is not a lack of piety or religious ritual. Verse 8 underscores how there are indeed priests, there are persons searching the Torah, and prophets presenting oracles. Israel is being religious. The problem, rather, is that their religious activity is masking the most fundamental question, "Where is the Lord?" Hence worship itself is attributed to Baal even though the rhetoric and liturgy may very well by Yahwistic.

The starting point for preaching Jeremiah 2:4-13 is to realize that it is a critique of tradition. The opening accusations suggest that tradition can actually eliminate God from worship when religion replaces God as the object of worship. When this happens, the central question of worship, Where is the Lord!, is no longer the organizing power within the worshiping community. Verses 10-13 describe such a situation as resulting in two specific evils—one, the rejection of God, and two, the worship of tradition—both of which are sketched out with metaphors. The rejection of God is described as the loss of living water: "They have forsaken me, the fountain of living water." In place of living water, the worship of tradition is like digging out a cracked cistern: "And (they) dug out cisterns for themselves, cracked cisterns that can hold no water." The closing image underscores how the worship of tradition is form without substance, since it could never hold any water, much less be an active fountain. The preacher may wish to probe both how worship in the local congregation raises the central question, Where is the Lord! and in what ways worship obscures it.

The Response: *Psalm 81:1, 10-16*

A Divine Proclamation

Setting. Psalm 81 was most likely part of a larger ritual meant for one of Israel's central festival days. Note the reference to "our festal day" in v. 3 and the location of this day "at the new moon." The form-critical designation of the psalm is difficult to determine. It begins with a hymnic mood. Note the call to praise in vv. 1-3 and the reasons for it in vv. 4-5. But the psalm switches to prophetic discourse at the close of v. 5 with the words, "I hear a voice not known." This rubric provides the point of transition to a divine oracle for the remainder of the psalm. Thus what begins as a festival hymn gives way to a divine speech.

Structure. Psalm 81 separates into two parts, the hymn in vv. 1-5*b* and the divine oracle in vv. 5*c*-16. Two rubrics provide clues for organizing the second half of the psalm. They occur in v. 5*c*, "I hear a voice I had not known" and in v. 10*c*, "Open your mouth wide and I will fill it." The first rubric appears to be the voice of the psalmist, which then provides transition to a divine oracle. The second rubric is the voice of God, most likely addressing the psalmist. If both are interpreted as introductions then the second half of the psalm would divide between vv. 5*c*-10*b* and 10*c*-16. The first section (vv. 5*c*-10*b*) is a recounting of God's salvation and the second (vv. 10*c*-16) traces Israel's rejection of it. Such a division indicates that the lectionary reading has cut across two sections in combining vv. 10-16, and that the self-identification of God in v. 10 is meant to function as the conclusion to vv. 5*c*-9 rather than as the introduction to vv. 11-16. In view of this the liturgist may wish to expand the response to include the entire divine oracle in vv. 5*c*-16.

Significance. The focus in the psalm, on the divine oracle breaking in somewhat suddenly into a worship setting of praise, provides an excellent counterpoint to the Old Testament lesson, where the worship of tradition excluded the central question, Where is the

Lord? In Psalm 81 God answers the question through self-revelation. The use of this psalm with its emphasis on theophany in the midst of religious festival allows the worshiping community to move beyond the accusations of Jeremiah 2:4-13.

New Testament Texts

Hebrews calls for specific actions as the letter moves to its conclusion with an admonition to "mutual love." The mutual love of Christians is itself given a clear theological basis with references to the angels, God, Scripture, and Jesus Christ. The Gospel lesson from Luke recalls another Sabbath setting in which Jesus performed a controversial healing and, then, taught his listeners, including especially the Pharisees, about humility and generosity that are in keeping with God's standards.

The Lesson: *Hebrews 13:1-8, 15-16*

The Form and Foundation of Mutual Love

Setting. The final section of Hebrews is the thirteenth chapter (13:1-25), which largely repeats the points and admonitions of the preceding chapters of the work. Our reading is typical of the themes and tone of the whole of Hebrews. The author issues practical admonitions about life and weaves a commanding theological thread through the advice. Indeed, one should see that the life-style advocated here is founded upon, even made possible by, the reality of Jesus Christ's presence in the lives of believers.

Structure. The author states so many particular points and laces these with theological and christological remarks that discerning the structure may at first seem baffling. In one way, however, the opening imperative of 13:1 summarized the theme of all of vv. 1-8. After this thematic admonition, vv. 2-3 call for hospitality and care for those in dire situations. At the heart of the directions is a statement about angels that underwrites the instructions. Then, v. 4 calls for faithfulness in marriage, and a statement about God's judgment explains the importance of fidelity. Next, vv. 5-6 call for a proper regard for money and possessions; here, two scriptural words about the Lord's promise of care offer security beyond material goods. In turn, vv. 7-8 direct the readers to look to their leaders as models of faithful living, and a christological declaration about the constancy of Jesus Christ underscores the eternal model for Christian living that guides, unifies, and enables life. Finally, vv. 15-16 expand on the role of Jesus Christ in Christian life and tell of God's desire for our lives.

Significance. Hebrews is a call to a life of bold faith. That central concern informs every section of the letter, and one finds a key to comprehending the author's statements in relating the remarks to a life of faith. Faith, according to Hebrews, gives shape to the lives of Christians. Our lesson ponders this truth in a variety of ways. The moral maxims of this reading are well summarized in the simple opening, "Let mutual love continue." The author continues by discussing "mutual love" in the appropriate terms of hospitality, care for the incarcerated and abused, marriage, greed and contentment, and leadership. Consistently, in terms of the various topics registered here, believers are reminded that they live in relation to others. Indeed, the Christian life portrayed in this text is a life characterized by care, concern, purity, fidelity, freedom, generosity, and loyalty.

Frequently New Testament writings create seemingly abstract lists of such desirable qualities, but Hebrews handles the matter more concretely. The vivid language is consistent with the author's understanding of faith—faith is a dynamic way of life, not merely following set patterns or rules. Faith is the result of believers' real relationships to God; it is living toward God that moves ever onward. Yet, as the text demonstrates with the references to angels, God, the Lord, and Jesus Christ, the faithful life of mutual Christian love is rooted in, founded upon, and motivated by the divine. We live toward God because God calls us forth.

We should see that faith informs existence. Indeed, faith forms life itself. Not everything goes. In relation to God and to others there are things Christians do and there are things that Christians do not do. Faith without form is as illegitimate as form without fiber or shape without substance. Hebrews does not catalogue the rules of Christianity, but our reading for this week directs us into a definite life of mutual love that has its origin and impetus in our relationship to God. In our relationship with Christ, our lives are focused in such a way that our actions find favor with God. As we live into Christ, our lives take on the character of God's own pleasure.

The Gospel: *Luke 14:1, 7-14*

Humility and Generosity That Are Godly

Setting. The lesson tells of Jesus' teaching at a banquet held by a leader among the Pharisees. The initial, isolated line (v. 1) establishes the setting: Jesus dines at the home of a prominent Pharisee on a Sabbath, and "they"—that is, the Pharisees—were watching him.

The main part of our lesson (vv. 7-14) comes after a leap over five crucial verses. In the context of this Sabbath banquet at which Jesus was being carefully observed by the Pharisees, Jesus healed a man afflicted by serious swelling. Thus, the atmosphere is similar to that reported by Luke in the lesson for last Sunday. Yet, here, instead of merely reporting Jesus' silencing words to his critics, Luke continues to recall Jesus' parabolic teaching about social order and God's regard for human social structures.

Structure. The lesson falls into three clear parts. First, v. 1 established the context of the Sabbath and the way the Pharisees "kept an eye on" Jesus. The lesson jumps over the controversial healing, but one should recognize that Jesus' words and the silencing of his adversaries are presupposed by the ensuing lines of our lesson. The second section of our lesson comes in vv. 7-11 with Jesus' parable to those at the banquet. The situational application of the story is easily apparent. Then, in vv. 12-14 we encounter the final portion of the lesson—a direct statement of instruction to Jesus' host with overt explanation of the theological reasons for the remarks.

Significance. The story focuses on Jesus: Jesus the scrutinized guest, Jesus the confrontational guest, and Jesus the teaching guest. The lesson is, however, more didactic than christological. From Jesus' words we learn primarily about God's standards of evaluation, and these, in turn, provide clear challenge to our lives.

There are several helpful ways to think about this text in relation to our own lives. Like the Pharisees we are curious about Jesus. Perhaps we do not have the suspicion or hostility that Luke would have us attribute to them, but we do come to passages such as this one to scrutinize Jesus' words and deeds. Are they credible? Do they have anything to do with our lives? If so, what and why? The story invites us into lively dialogue with the words and ways of Jesus. Thus, we struggle with what the story meant and with what it means.

Unlike the modest banquet guest in Jesus' story, however, we do not tend to take the lowly seat; rather, we typically clamor for attention and actively seek the place of honor in life. Our culture has told us and trained us to "go for it," to "fulfill ourselves" so that we can be whole and healthy human beings. Putting others ahead of ourselves sounds psychologically unhealthy to people formed by the world today. Yet, Jesus calls us to take on a different set of standards from those offered to us by the world; we are to live our lives in keeping with the standards of God. We are to ignore the way this world operates and recognize that God's love is equally applicable to all humans—rich and poor, prominent and marginal.

God's ways are not ours. We give to get, but God gives to those who cannot give back (as well as to those who could if they would or can if they will). Jesus tells his audience and us that we are called to live in relation to others as God lives in relation to us. No human has any claim on God. Whatever we have comes to us out of God's pure grace. Thus, we should recognize God's grace with gratitude and live with genuine humility. We do not do God's will by becoming falsely humble in order to posture ourselves into God's recognition. In turn, as we live humbly, recognizing God's unmerited gifts to us, we become naturally generous; for as we recognize all the good that comes to us by God's grace, we will become agents of that same grace in relation to others. To acknowledge in humility that we live by grace frees us and energizes us to live generously or graciously as an expression of our gratitude. In other words, to know who God is tells us who we are and motivates us to live the kind of life that God would have us live, as we know by knowing God.

True godliness is a reckless investment in the parts of the world that beg for attention in real need but that show no potential of paying back dividends. Yet, Jesus promises that God sees and that God will pay the interest on an investment in the vulnerable elements of humankind. The reference to the resurrection of the dead takes the thought of divine reward completely out of the context of our present existence. Does this teaching mean that we give to get, only at a later date and in a bigger way? No, for there is no manipulating grace; yet, Jesus assures us of God's approval and recognition of appropriate humility and generosity. A truly humble and truly generous person will not be tempted to force God's grace, but such persons have the divine assurance of God's active and ultimate approval of their lives. The old promise of pie-in-the-sky-by-and-by functioned to keep disenfranchised and oppressed people happy, to keep them from claiming in the present world what they understood to be God's intentions for their lives. Jesus' words work in exactly the opposite fashion. Talk of God's future should not keep us passive, rather we should be moved in the present by Jesus' speaking about God's future to take action to live humble and generous lives.

Proper 17: The Celebration

The Gospel reading presents an opportunity to discuss the virtue of humility in relation to the text, "For all who exalt themselves will be humbled, and those who humble themselves will be exalted." The fact that this text appears with little variation at least ten times in the Gospels suggests how deeply ingrained it must have been in the mind of the primitive Church and that it must have been a constant theme in the preaching of the historical Jesus.

While preachers are able to excoriate the deadly sin of pride with vigor, they have difficulty with its opposite number, the godly virtue of humility. Unfortunately, to expel the demon pride does not mean that the angel humility will move right in. Other demons may stake a claim. Whether it be the demon greed with its substitution of possessions for self-worth or the demon sloth choosing a life of comfort now because it has no hope for the future, both will have an eye on the beachfront property that is the human soul.

The difficulty we may have with talking about humility is not only our consciousness that the disposition of the culture is counter to it, but our awareness that it can vanish if we become too absorbed in it. Self-conscious humility ("I thank God for my humility," says

Gloucester in *Richard III*) soon is metamorphosed into pride. And humility has sometimes suffered at the hands of its advocates by being presented as a form of self-abasement that does not ring true to the other scriptural affirmation that we are made in God's image.

Today's lessons suggest one way of interpreting the virtue of humility for a contemporary Christian audience. Pride is understood in the lesson from Jeremiah as our insistence on digging broken cisterns for ourselves, as worshiping the traditions of our own devising. The lesson from Hebrews shows of what true humility consists, a selflessness on behalf of others that is based in the eternal self-giving nature of Christ. And the Gospel lesson can suggest to us that in the eucharistic feast, the bridal feast of the Lamb, we demonstrate how *agape* is the manifestation of true humility. We are not humbled to make a statement about ourselves; humility is an attitude of service in reference to the world which we derive from our incorporation into the Body of Christ. It is interesting in this regard to note that the collects of the 1979 *Book of Common Prayer* (eg., pp. 211, 214, 219) will refer to Christ's humility, but they do not put into the mouth of the Church comments about its own humility.

A suggested sermon hymn based on the theme of humility expressed through service is "Lord, Whose Love Through [in] Humble Service," to be found in the recent hymnals of the Brethren and Mennonite (no. 369), Episcopalian (no. 610), Lutheran (no. 423), Presbyterian (no. 427), and United Methodist (no. 581), and in the non-denominational *Hymns for the Living Church* (no. 512).

Scripture Index

Old Testament

159

A Comparison of Major Lectionaries

YEAR C: TIME AFTER PENTECOST
(TRINITY SUNDAY AND PROPERS 6-17)

	Old Testament	Psalm	Epistle	Gospel
		TRINITY SUNDAY		
RCL	Prov. 8:1-4, 22-31	8	Rom. 5:1-5	John 16:12-15
RoCath	Prov. 8:22-31	8:4-9		
Episcopal	Isa. 6:1-8	29	Rev. 4:1-11	John 16:(5-11) 12-15
Lutheran	Prov. 8:22-31			

		PROPER 6 (June 12-18)		
		[RC: 11th Ordinary time]	[Luth: 4th After Pent.]	
RCL	I Kings 21:1-10 (11-14), 15-21a	5:1-8	Gal. 2:15-21	Luke 7:36–8:3
RoCath	II Sam. 12:7-10, 13	32:1-2, 5, 7, 11	Gal. 2:16, 19-21	
Episcopal	II Sam. 11:26–12:10, 13-15	32	Gal. 2:11-21	Luke 7:36-50
Lutheran	II Sam. 11:26–12:10, 13-15	32	Gal. 2:11-21	Luke 7:36-50

PROPER 7 (June 19-25)

[RC: 12th Ordinary Time] [Luth: 5th After Pent.]

RCL	I Kings 19:1-4 (5-7), 8-15a	42, 43	Gal. 3:23-29	Luke 8:26-39
RoCath	Zech. 12:10-11	63:2-6, 8-9	Gal. 3:26-29	Luke 9:18-24
Episcopal	Zech. 12:8-10; 13:1	63:1-8		Luke 9:18-24
Lutheran	Zech. 12:7-10	63:1-8		Luke 9:18-24

PROPER 8 (June 26–July 2)

[RC: 13th Ordinary Time] [Luth: 6th After Pent.]

RCL	II Kings 2:1-2, 6-14	77:1-2, 11-20	Gal. 5:1, 13-25	Luke 9:51-62
RoCath	I Kings 19:16-21	16:1-2, 5, 7-11	Gal. 5:1, 13-18	
Episcopal	I Kings 19:15-16, 19-21	16		
Lutheran	I Kings 19:14-21	16		

PROPER 9 (July 3-9)
[RC: 14th Ordinary Time]   [Luth: 7th After Pent.]

RCL	II Kings 5:1-14	30	Gal. 6:(1-6) 7-16	Luke 10:1-11, 16-20
RoCath	Isa. 66:10-14	66:1-7, 16, 20	Gal. 6:14-18	Luke 10:1-12, 17-20
Episcopal	Isa. 66:10-16	66	Gal. 6:(1-10), 14-18	Luke 10:1-12, 16-20
Lutheran	Isa. 66:10-14	66:1-11, 14-18	Gal. 6:1-10, 14-16	Luke 10:1-12, 16 (17-20)

PROPER 10 (July 10-16)
[RC: 15th Ordinary Time]   [Luth: 8th After Pent.]

RCL	Amos 7:7-17	82	Col. 1:1-14	Luke 10:25-37
RoCath	Deut. 30:10-14	69:14-17, 30-31, 33-34, 36-37	Col. 1:15-20	
Episcopal	Deut. 30:9-14	25		
Lutheran	Deut. 30:9-14	25:1-9		

PROPER 11 (July 17-23)
[RC: 16th Ordinary Time]   [Luth: 9th After Pent.]

RCL	Amos 8:1-12	52	Col. 1:15-28	Luke 10:38-42
RoCath	Gen. 18:1-10	15:2-5	Col. 1:24-28	
Episcopal	Gen. 18:1-10a (10b-14)	15	Col. 1:21-29	
Lutheran	Gen. 18:1-10a, (10b-14)	15	Col. 1:21-28	

PROPER 12 (July 24-30)
[RC: 17th Ordinary Time]   [Luth: 10th After Pent.]

RCL	Hosea 1:2-10	85	Col. 2:6-15	Luke 11:1-13
RoCath	Gen. 18:20-32	138:1-3, 6-8	Col. 2:12-14	
Lutheran	Gen. 18:20-33	138	Col. 2:6-15	
Lutheran	Gen. 18:20-32	138	Col. 2:6-15	

PROPER 13 (July 31–Aug. 6)
[RC: 18th Ordinary Time]   [Luth: 11th After Pent.]

RCL	Hosea 11:1-11	107:1-9, 43	Col. 3:1-11	Luke 12:13-21
RoCath	Eccl. 1:2; 2:21-23	95:1-2, 6-9	Col. 3:1-5, 9-11	
Episcopal	Eccl. 1:12-14; 2:(1-7, 11) 18-23	49	Col. 3:(5-11) 12-17	
Lutheran	Eccl. 1:2; 2:18-26	49:1-11		

PROPER 14 (Aug. 7-13)
[RC: 19th Ordinary Time] [Luth: 12th After Pent.]

RCL	Isa. 1:1, 10-20	50:1-8, 22-23	Heb. 11:1-3, 8-16	Luke 12:32-40
RoCath	Wisdom 18:6-9	33:1, 12, 18-22	Heb. 11:1-2, 8-19	Luke 12:32-48
Episcopal	Gen. 15:1-6	33	Heb. 11:1-3 (4-7),	
Lutheran	Gen. 15:1-6	33	8-16	

PROPER 15 (Aug. 14-20)
[RC: 20th Ordinary Time] [Luth: 13th after Pent.]

RCL	Isa. 5:1-7	80:1-2, 8-19	Heb:11:29–12:2	Luke 12:49-56
RoCath	Jer. 38:4-6, 8-10	40:2-4, 18	Heb: 12:1-4	Luke 12:49-53
Episcopal	Jer. 23:23-29	82	Heb. 12:1-7 (8-10), 11-14	
Lutheran	Jer. 23:23-29	82	Heb. 12:1-13	Luke 12:49-53

PROPER 16 (Aug. 21-27)
[RC: 21st Ordinary Time] [Luth: 14th After Pent.]

RCL	Jer. 1:4-10	71:1-6	Heb. 12:18-29	Luke 13:10-17
RoCath	Isa. 66:18-21	117	Heb. 12:5-7, 11-13	Luke 13:22-30
Episcopal	Isa. 28:14-22	46	Heb. 12:18-19, 22-29	Luke 13:22-30
Lutheran	Isa. 66:18-23	117	Heb. 12:18-24	Luke 13:22-30

PROPER 17 (Aug. 28–Sept. 3)
[RC: 22nd Ordinary Time]   [Luth: 15th After Pent.]

RCL	Jer. 2:4-13	81:1, 10-16	Heb. 13:1-8, 15-16	Luke 14:1, 7-14
RoCath	Sir. 3:17-18, 20, 28-29	68:4-7, 10-11	Heb. 12:18-19, 22-24	
Episcopal	Ecclus. 10:(7-11),	112	Heb. 13:1-8	
Lutheran	Prov. 25:6-7	112	Heb. 13:1-8	

167

A Liturgical Calendar

Trinity Sunday Through August 1993–2001

	1993 A	1994 B	1995 C	1996 A	1997 B
Trinity	June 6	May 29	June 11	June 2	May 25
Proper 4					June 1
Proper 5		June 5		June 9	June 8
Proper 6	June 13	June 12	June 18	June 16	June 15
Proper 7	June 20	June 19	June 25	June 23	June 22
Proper 8	June 27	June 26	July 2	June 30	June 29
Proper 9	July 4	July 3	July 9	July 7	July 6
Proper 10	July 11	July 10	July 16	July 14	July 13
Proper 11	July 18	July 17	July 23	July 21	July 20
Proper 12	July 25	July 24	July 30	July 28	July 27
Proper 13	Aug. 1	July 31	Aug. 6	Aug. 4	Aug. 3
Proper 14	Aug. 8	Aug. 7	Aug. 13	Aug. 11	Aug. 10
Proper 15	Aug. 15	Aug. 14	Aug. 20	Aug. 18	Aug. 17
Proper 16	Aug. 22	Aug. 21	Aug. 27	Aug. 25	Aug. 24
Proper 17	Aug. 29	Aug. 28	Sept. 3	Sept. 1	Aug. 31

	1998	1999	2000	2001
	C	A	B	C
Trinity	June 7	May 30	June 18	June 10
Proper 4	———	———	———	———
Proper 5	———	June 6	———	———
Proper 6	June 14	June 13	———	June 17
Proper 7	June 21	June 20	June 25	June 24
Proper 8	June 28	June 27	July 2	July 1
Proper 9	July 5	July 4	July 9	July 8
Proper 10	July 12	July 11	July 16	July 15
Proper 11	July 19	July 18	July 23	July 22
Proper 12	July 26	July 25	July 30	July 29
Proper 13	Aug. 2	Aug. 7	Aug. 6	Aug. 5
Proper 14	Aug. 9	Aug. 8	Aug. 13	Aug. 12
Proper 15	Aug. 16	Aug. 15	Aug. 20	Aug. 19
Proper 16	Aug. 23	Aug. 22	Aug. 27	Aug. 26
Proper 17	Aug. 30	Aug. 29	Sept. 3	Sept. 2